LOS AN[GELES]

NEIGHBOURHOODS

C000199215

LOS FELIZ

HOLLYWOOD

BEVERLY HILLS

SILVER LAKE

DOWNTOWN L.A

[V]ENICE

INGLEWOOD

LOS ANGELES

CULT RECIPES

Los Angeles
CULT RECIPES

VICTOR GARNIER ASTORINO

MURDOCH BOOKS

SYDNEY · LONDON

BETH. ELECTRIC AVE & CALIFORNIA AVE

CONTENTS

INTRODUCTION

'Dear Victor, parts 12 and 16 of your report are not relevant to the topic. You do understand that this is a reflection on your academic experience and not a travel guide. Kindly remove these sections.'

It was with these stinging words that the academic dean of my school received the report of my university exchange to Los Angeles in 2010. Too many photos of hamburgers! And yet as soon as I returned, still obsessed with this subject, I started working on opening a gourmet burger restaurant in Paris. I dreamed it, created it, called it Blend Hamburger, and it saw the day in late 2011. I was quickly joined by my partner, accomplice and friend Adrian, without whom no page of this book could have been written, and since then we make sure we each eat at least one hamburger a day. Six years later, when this Los Angeles travel diary was proposed, life gave me the opportunity to bring my two passions together: cooking and photography. An amazing fate for what was once seen as 'off topic'! Even better, it was in the city that has always pushed me to do what I love.

To carry out this project, I chose to go alone and take only my analogue cameras. Not being able to see the shots before I went back to France made each moment last much longer, and now, with the developed film I take precious care of the material trace of this total immersion. I will never, for example, forget my dinner with Richard, who invited me to join him at his table because there was a 45-minute wait at Little Dom's for its spaghetti and meatballs, and night was falling. In the end, the photo was ruined ... If I had known at the time, I'm not sure I would have had such a good time.

In Los Angeles, no door is ever closed. Wherever I was, and even when it was not a good time, I was always given a chance. I didn't receive a single negative response from anyone I approached. I feel like once you throw yourself (or lose yourself) in something that makes you happy, people don't judge you, whatever it is. This is a city that lets people live their dream.

This dream is everywhere. It is in the manners and attitudes ... It is also at the heart of its economy, as Los Angeles lives to the beat of the film, television and music industry. It works itself into the diversity of its landscapes: from the enormous freeways I spent so many hours on, to the heights of Hollywood, where a few minutes' walk takes you outside of civilisation. And it fully comes into its own on the Pacific Coast Highway, which runs alongside the massive, powerful and omnipresent ocean …

All of these elements that inspire dreams and meditation surely explain why Los Angeles is home to some of the most creative and healthy food in the world. The menus of the restaurants seem totally freed from convention. It is also perhaps the meeting of the city's many cultures, combined with certain American eating habits, that produces these extraordinary ideas. Only in Los Angeles, for example, is it normal to eat a Thai pizza or order a Korean taco.

The quest for wellbeing fosters their creativity. Alex, the co-founder of Caffe' Delfini, told me the idea of serving julienned zucchini (courgette) with his bolognese sauce was as a replacement for high-calorie spaghetti. So some of the most delicious, non-conformist dishes in this food diary start from the imperative to do oneself good, without dogma or limits.

The shared, unbendable rule of this game, the safeguard of all these ideas, is the worship of local produce, elevated to the level of the sacred. The restaurants effectively develop a sacred bond with their local environment, in particular through the farmers' markets, their preferred source of supply. The city's nickname in fact is 'the farm of the United States', because of the diversity and volume of its agricultural production. The possibilities on restaurant menus are limitless.

This book of cult recipes pays tribute to the Angelenos and the incredible fecundity of Los Angeles, both for the body and the mind. I hope it will help persuade you to go and discover or rediscover the City of Angels, and especially to taste the original versions of these dishes, some of which seem straight out of a dream to me.

Chap. 1
WEST LOS ANGELES
SANTA MONICA
BRENTWOOD
SAWTELLE

HICKORY BURGER WITH CHEESE

SERVES 4

Grapeseed oil

Fine sea salt

500 g (1 lb 2 oz) minced (ground) beef

2 teaspoons liquid smoke (American food stores)

8 cheddar cheese slices

4 hamburger buns

4 tablespoons mayonnaise

1 large pickle (gherkin)

1 iceberg lettuce

2 teaspoons Smoky tomato sauce (page 258)

In a hot frying pan brushed with grapeseed oil, cook four seasoned minced beef patties over medium heat on one side for 3 minutes. Mix together 150 ml (5 fl oz) water and the liquid smoke. Pour a quarter of the mixture onto each burger. The frying pan must be hot enough for the water to evaporate immediately. Flip the burgers and arrange two slices of cheddar in a star shape on each burger. For a rare burger, keep cooking for another 3 minutes; for medium, 4 minutes; for well done, 5 minutes. To assemble the burger: spread the bottom half of the bun with mayonnaise, then add rounds of pickle, three to four lettuce leaves cut to the width of the hamburger, the burger with the melted cheese and the smoky tomato sauce, then top with the other half of the bun.

What a pleasure to eat at The Apple Pan! Despite the fact you often have to queue and you can't stay forever because you have to give up your seat. It is one of the oldest restaurants in Los Angeles. The sodas are still served in paper cones, just like in the 1940s. And the smoky flavour of their hickory burger remains a secret that many fans would dream of decoding. My version, which is not the restaurant's, reveals an accessible technique that brings us closer to that unique flavour.

1970 PLYMOUTH HEMI CUDA, CARS WITH CLASS, WILSHIRE BLVD SANTA MONICA

OLD-FASHIONED APPLE PIE

MAKES 1 PIE

THE PASTRY
400 g (14 oz/2⅔ cups) plain (all-purpose) flour
200 g (7 oz) butter, cut into cubes
30 ml (1 fl oz) iced water

THE APPLES
1.4 kg (3 lb 2 oz) apples
125 g (4½ oz) caster (superfine) sugar
2 pinches cinnamon, plus extra to sprinkle
1 pinch ground nutmeg
45 g (1½ oz) plain (all-purpose) flour
2 tablespoons lemon juice
1 pinch coarse salt
50 g (1¾ oz) butter
1 egg yolk
2 tablespoons soft brown sugar

For the pastry: blend the flour with 1 teaspoon salt in a food processor. Add the butter and pulse until mixed evenly but not pasty. Add the iced water, little by little, continuing to mix in short bursts. Shape the dough into two flattened rounds and place them in the refrigerator in two plastic bags for 45 minutes. Preheat the oven to 220°C (425°F). Roll each pastry round out to a circle 5 mm (¼ inch) thick, one with a diameter 5 cm (2 inches) larger than the edge of the pie dish for the base, the other 5 cm (2 inches) smaller for the top crust. For the apples: cut the apples into medium-sized slices and mix well with the sugar, 2 pinches of salt, the spices, flour and lemon juice. Let this mixture rest for 10 minutes. Sprinkle with the coarse salt. Lay the larger circle of pastry in the bottom of the pie dish, pour the apple mixture onto the pastry, cut the butter into small cubes and dot over the apples. Cover with the other circle of pastry and seal the edges by pressing them with a fork. Brush the pastry with the egg yolk. Sprinkle with the brown sugar and a little cinnamon. Cut slits in the top two thirds of the way down. Cook the pie in the lower part of the oven for 30 minutes at 220°C (425°F). Reduce the temperature to 180°C (350°F) and cook for a further 45 minutes, covered with foil.

1963 FORD RANCHERO, ABBOT KINNEY BLVD & N VENICE BLVD

CORA'S COFFEE SHOPPE

CHICKEN BREAKFAST BURRITO

MAKES 4 BURRITOS
4 large tortillas (wheat or corn)
1 avocado
8 cheddar cheese slices
80 g (2¾ oz) crème fraîche or
sour cream
Fresh fruit, to serve
SCRAMBLED EGGS
8 eggs
15 g (½ oz) butter
45 ml (1½ fl oz) thin (pouring/whipping)
cream
MEXICAN RICE
280 g (10 oz) rice
20 ml (½ fl oz) grapeseed oil
320 g (11¼ oz) tomatoes
70 g (2½ oz) onion
Coriander (cilantro), to taste
CHICKEN
400 g (14 oz) skinless chicken breast
fillets
25 ml (¾ fl oz) olive oil

Scrambled eggs: whisk the eggs and season with salt and freshly ground black pepper. Cook the eggs for at least 5 minutes in a hot frying pan greased with butter. Add the cream to stop the cooking process and mix in. For the Mexican rice: wash the rice three times and drain well. Heat the oil in a saucepan and brown the rice for 3 minutes, stirring, on a high heat. Blend the tomatoes in a food processor with 300 ml (10½ fl oz) water, the chopped onion and some salt until smooth, at least 2 minutes. Once the rice has browned, reduce the heat to medium and add the puréed tomato and coriander. Once the liquid has reduced down to the level of the rice, cover and cook for 2 minutes. Let it rest for at least 20 minutes. For the chicken: season the chicken on all sides with salt and pepper. Drizzle with olive oil and bake on a baking tray at 180°C (350°F) for 18 minutes. Heat the tortillas on a medium heat in a lightly oiled frying pan for 3 minutes. Make a layer of Mexican rice in the middle of the burrito, add some cold, shredded chicken, thin slices of avocado, scrambled eggs, two cheddar cheese slices, and spread with crème fraîche. To assemble: fold two opposing sides of the burrito inwards and then roll it up starting from an unfolded side. Brown the burrito by rolling it in the hot frying pan for about 2 minutes. Cut in half and serve with fresh fruit.

20TH & OLYMPIC BLVD

BUCKWHEAT BLUEBERRY PANCAKES

MAKES 4 PANCAKES
50 g (1¾ oz/⅓ cup) plain (all-purpose) flour
200 g (7 oz/1½ cups) buckwheat flour
½ teaspoon baking powder
½ teaspoon bicarbonate of soda (baking soda)
2 eggs
75 ml (2¼ fl oz) milk
375 ml (13 fl oz/1½ cups) buttermilk
45 g (1½ oz) melted butter, plus extra for frying
½ pinch salt
2 teaspoons sugar
1 handful blueberries
Maple syrup, to serve

Quickly mix all of the ingredients together, except the blueberries and maple syrup. Do not overmix or the batter might thicken. Pour a ladleful of batter into a frying pan brushed with a little butter. Add the blueberries and cook for 2 minutes on a medium heat until bubbles appear in the pancake. Turn over and cook for 1 more minute. Serve with the maple syrup.

It was at Cora's that I first discovered that, as well as being delicious, a burrito can also be an excellent breakfast (see previous page), especially before a big day. Even at 7 am, their garden patio is sometimes packed.

LA URBAN FITNESS NUTRITION CENTER
MUSCLE BEACH VENICE SMOOTHIE

MAKES 1 SMOOTHIE
240 ml (8 fl oz) fresh almond milk
1 frozen banana
1 small handful frozen raspberries
1 small handful frozen blueberries
1 small handful frozen blackberries
1 scoop vanilla flavour plant protein
powder (organic food stores)
1 scoop green superfood powder
(organic food stores)
1 scoop BCAA (essential amino acid food
supplement)*
1 scoop amino acid powder*
1 scoop creatine powder*
1 scoop glutamine powder*
*specialty fitness stores

Blend all the ingredients together in a food processor for
2 minutes. Serve well chilled.

*A few steps from Muscle Beach, the LA Urban Fitness Nutrition
Center is a temple, not only of bodybuilding, but also wellbeing,
with one of the most comprehensive juice bars in Los Angeles.*

PINKBERRY
FROZEN YOGHURT

MAKES 6 YOGHURTS
1.2 kg (2 lb 12 oz) Greek-style yoghurt (non-fat)
320 ml (11 fl oz) low-fat milk
75 g (2½ oz) caster (superfine) sugar
15 ml (½ fl oz) agave syrup
1 teaspoon natural vanilla extract
30 ml (1 fl oz) fresh lemon juice
1 big handful strawberries, to serve
1 handful blueberries, to serve
1 handful pomegranate seeds, to serve
1 handful Granola (page 196), to serve

Mix together the yoghurt, milk, sugar and agave syrup until the mixture is smooth and the sugar has dissolved. Add the vanilla and lemon juice. Mix together. Pour into the bowl of an ice cream machine and follow the instructions. Serve immediately for a very smooth and creamy texture (or take it out of the freezer 15 minutes before serving). Add the cut fruit or granola when serving.

I always find it very hard to settle sensibly for one or two fresh fruits and some cereal when I am faced with the full array of Pinkberry toppings. Each one is more tempting than the last. This is however the best way to enjoy Pinkberry's non-fat frozen yoghurt. They were the first to establish themselves in Los Angeles in 2005.

4TH & BROADWAY, SANTA MONICA

SANTA MONICA SEAFOOD

CIOPPINO (FISH & SEAFOOD STEW)

SERVES 2

2½ tablespoons chopped basil
4 tablespoons olive oil
10 clams (vongole)
10 mussels
4 garlic cloves
40 g (1½ oz) French shallots, chopped
1 teaspoon chilli flakes
185 ml (6 fl oz/¾ cup) white wine
125 ml (4 fl oz/½ cup) fish stock made
with water and 1 fish stock cube
120 g (4¼ oz) firm white fish
10 prawns (shrimp)
50 g (1¾ oz) crabmeat
2 tablespoons chopped parsley
4 slices artisan-style bread, toasted
TOMATO SAUCE
½ celery stalk
1 onion
Olive oil
½ teaspoon sugar
½ teaspoon onion powder
½ teaspoon chilli flakes
½ teaspoon oregano
300 g (10½ oz) fresh tomatoes
100 g (3½ oz) tomato paste
(concentrated tomato purée)

Make the tomato sauce in a saucepan: sauté the chopped celery and chopped onion in 2 tablespoons olive oil on a medium heat for 5 minutes. Add the sugar, onion powder, chilli flakes, oregano, 2½ teaspoons salt and ½ teaspoon freshly ground black pepper. Cook for another 5 minutes, stirring all the time. Add the diced fresh tomatoes with the tomato paste. Cook for 5 minutes, stirring. Reduce the heat and cook, covered, for 15 minutes. Put ½ tablespoon of the basil and 2 tablespoons of the olive oil in a frying pan on a high heat. Add the clams and mussels. Crush two of the garlic cloves and add those, along with the chopped shallots, 2½ teaspoons salt and the chilli flakes. Sauté for 3–4 minutes, stirring constantly. Add the wine and reduce for 3 minutes. Add the fish stock, stir well and cook for 4 minutes. Add 230 g (8 oz) of the tomato sauce, along with the fish, prawns and crabmeat. When the fish is cooked, serve with the parsley, remaining basil and two slices of toasted bread rubbed with the remaining halved garlic cloves and drizzled with the remaining olive oil.

It was a ritual: my friend Aymeric, who lived in LA, and I would go once a week to Santa Monica Seafood for its lobster roll and swordfish sliders. Spending an afternoon with Stefani, I realised the full extent of their activities and understood why they are leaders in their field. They play a pioneering role with their policy of controlled and responsible fishing.

SANTA MONICA SEAFOOD

LOBSTER ROLL

SERVES 2

1 fresh lobster or 300 g (10½ oz) frozen
or tinned lobster meat
40 g (1½ oz) butter
2 tablespoons light crème fraîche (or
light sour cream)
20 ml (½ fl oz) lemon juice
1 teaspoon grated lemon zest
2 garlic cloves
200 g (7 oz) mayonnaise
½ bunch chives
2 hot dog buns
French fries, to serve

Cook the lobster in a large pot of boiling salted water for
6 minutes, adding the claws half way through the cooking
time. Remove all of the meat and drain. Sauté the cooked
meat for 3–5 minutes in a frying pan on a medium heat with
half the butter; the lobster flesh should be golden. Whip the
light crème fraîche with the lemon juice and zest, then add
the crushed garlic and beat for 2 minutes. Gradually incorporate
this mixture into the mayonnaise. Season with ½ teaspoon
salt and ½ teaspoon freshly ground black pepper and add the
chopped chives. Set aside in the refrigerator for at least 1 hour.
Add the lobster to the sauce and mix together well. Split open
the hot dog buns and heat them in a 180°C (350°F) oven for
3 minutes, then fill the buns with the lobster mixture. Serve
with French fries.

SANTA MONICA SEAFOOD
SWORDFISH SLIDERS

MAKES 3 SLIDERS

1 carrot

1 onion

A few white cabbage leaves

1 teaspoon mustard

2 tablespoons mayonnaise

½ teaspoon sugar

2 tablespoons olive oil

3 small swordfish fillets

White pepper

3 mini hamburger (slider) buns

Chipotle aïoli (page 258)

1 tomato, sliced

3 cornichons (baby gherkins)

French fries, to serve

Julienne the carrot, finely chop the onion and finely shred the cabbage leaves. Mix together the mustard, mayonnaise and sugar. Add the mayonnaise sauce to the vegetables and mix together well. Heat the olive oil in a hot frying pan on a medium heat and cook the swordfish fillets for 3–4 minutes on each side; the surface should be golden brown. Season with the white pepper just before the end of the cooking time. Toast the halved hamburger buns for 3 minutes in a 180°C (350°F) oven. To assemble: spread the bottom halves of the buns with chipotle aïoli, then top with pan-fried swordfish fillets, a slice of tomato and some of the coleslaw. Top with the other half of the bun. Skewer a small cornichon on a toothpick and insert in the slider. Serve with French fries.

CHICKEN PAD SEE EW

SERVES 1

100 g (3½ oz) wide flat rice noodles
1 tablespoon vegetable oil
1 garlic clove
125 g (4½ oz) skinless chicken breast
fillets, cut into pieces
1 egg
½ teaspoon rice vinegar
½ teaspoon soy sauce
1½ tablespoons sugar
1 handful Chinese broccoli (gai larn)
½ teaspoon dark soy sauce
½ teaspoon oyster sauce
½ teaspoon fish sauce
1 pinch white pepper

Cook the noodles as directed on the packet. Pour the oil into a very hot frying pan. Add the chopped garlic and stir for about 30 seconds. Add the chicken and stir-fry for about 3 minutes, until browned. Add the cooked rice noodles and mix well. Add the egg and stir vigorously for about 2 minutes to coat all of the mixture. Add the rice vinegar, regular soy sauce and sugar, continuing to stir vigorously for about 2 minutes. Add the Chinese broccoli, dark soy sauce, oyster sauce and fish sauce and stir-fry for 1 minute. Finish with white pepper, and mix.

What an honour it was that Henry opened the doors of his kitchen to me and I could finally find out how to achieve this complex flavour. At the bottom of my apartment in Santa Monica, I crossed the threshold of this Thai restaurant, family-run since 1986, countless times. This is the dish I miss most when I am in France, it is the taste of Los Angeles for me.

PRAWN PAD THAI

SERVES 1

100 g (3½ oz) wide flat rice noodles
1 tablespoon vegetable oil
1 garlic clove
5–7 large raw prawns (shrimp)
1 egg
1 teaspoon rice vinegar
1 tablespoon fish sauce
1½ tablespoons sugar
1 tablespoon peanuts
2 spring onions (scallions)
½ teaspoon paprika
1 handful bean sprouts
1 pinch white pepper
1 tablespoon lime juice

Cook the noodles as directed on the packet. Pour the vegetable oil into a hot wok and sauté the crushed garlic for 30 seconds, then add the peeled and deveined prawns. Cook for at least 3 minutes, until browned. Add the noodles. Mix together well. Add the egg and stir vigorously for about 2 minutes; the whole mixture needs to be coated. Add the rice vinegar, fish sauce and sugar and cook, stirring constantly, for about 2 minutes. Add the roughly crushed peanuts, sliced spring onions, paprika and bean sprouts. Stir-fry for 1 minute. Add the white pepper, stir-fry for a few seconds, take off the heat and sprinkle with lime juice.

VEGGIE GARDEN WRAP

MAKES 1 WRAP

1 carrot
1 zucchini (courgette)
Soy-ginger sauce (page 258)
40 g (1½ oz) brown rice
1 large corn tortilla
Butter, for greasing
60 g (2¼ oz) hummus
1 handful baby English spinach
½ avocado
¼ cos (romaine) lettuce
2 tomatoes
Tahini sauce (page 258)
Hot sauce, to serve

Cut the carrot and zucchini into sticks and cook them in boiling water. Drain. Add 60 ml (2 fl oz/¼ cup) of the soy-ginger sauce to the vegetables and keep them warm. Cook the rice according to the instructions on the packet. Heat the tortilla for 3 minutes in a frying pan greased with butter on a medium heat. Turn the tortilla over. To assemble the wrap: in the frying pan, off the heat, spread the tortilla with hummus and add the spinach, hot rice, pickled carrot and zucchini, sliced avocado, cos lettuce, and rounds of sliced tomato. Top with tahini sauce. Fold two edges of the tortilla inwards and roll up the wrap starting from one of the non-folded sides. Cut in half. Serve with hot sauce or what's left of the other sauces.

KALE PIZZA

MAKES 1 PIZZA
200 g (7 oz) kale
Olive oil
1 tablespoon lemon juice
½ onion
1 ball mozzarella cheese (125 g/4½ oz)
60 g (2¼ oz) fresh goat's cheese
1 pinch chilli powder
170 g (6 oz) Pizza dough (page 262)
½ handful pine nuts

Slice the kale and marinate it in 2 tablespoons olive oil and the lemon juice for at least 1 hour in the refrigerator. Preheat the oven to its hottest setting. Slice the half onion and caramelise it on a high heat in a frying pan brushed with olive oil for about 5 minutes, stirring. Season with salt and freshly ground black pepper. Dry the mozzarella with paper towel and cut it into six or eight pieces. Mix together the kale, goat's cheese, chilli powder and onion. Season. Spread the seasoned pizza dough with the kale mixture and arrange the mozzarella on top. Bake for 15–20 minutes until the edges are brown and the mozzarella is melted. Sprinkle with the pine nuts that have been toasted in a frying pan with a drizzle of olive oil on a high heat for 4 minutes, stirring well.

I met Bashar, one of the two happy owners of this restaurant, when I sat next to his daughter there, by chance. A real institution for Angelenos, this Brentwood neighbourhood restaurant manages the delicate balance of combining pleasure and wellbeing, with generous, luscious dishes that are also fresh and balanced.

BUTTERMILK BISCUIT WITH SUNNY-SIDE UP EGGS

SERVES 6

500 g (1 lb 2 oz) blueberries
115 g (4 oz) caster (superfine) sugar
25 ml (¾ fl oz) lemon juice
450 g (1 lb/3 cups) plain (all-purpose)
flour
20 g (¾ oz) bicarbonate of soda (baking
soda)
100 g (3½ oz) butter
14 eggs
265 ml (9½ fl oz) buttermilk
1 tablespoon milk
6 thick slices ham
Olive oil for frying

Preheat the oven to 175°C (345°F). Bring half the blueberries, 75 g (2½ oz) of the sugar and the lemon juice to the boil, stirring. Turn off the heat, add the remaining blueberries, stir well and cool. Mix the flour, 40 g (1½ oz) of the sugar, the bicarbonate of soda and 10 g (¼ oz) salt with the cubed butter. Whisk two eggs with the buttermilk. Combine the two mixtures and knead for 5 minutes. Flatten the dough on a floured work surface to a thickness of 1.5 cm (⅝ inch). Cut out 8 cm (3¼ inch) rounds using a cookie cutter. Mix two eggs with the milk and lightly brush the top of the rounds. Bake in the oven for 15 minutes. In a frying pan on a medium heat brushed with olive oil, brown the ham on each side for 2 minutes. Fry the remaining eggs, sunny side up, in the same frying pan. For the sandwich: open up the biscuit, spread each side with blueberry jam, and insert one slice of fried ham, folded in half. Serve with the two eggs.

I still have in my memory the handshake of Brian, the chef at Farmshop, and the smile of Sarah, the manager, as well as the spectacular energy that Farmshop devotes to innovation and making sure everything is good. There are always new things in their food store, and the same applies to their menu, which changes with the seasons and the rhythm of what's available at the local farmers' markets, their only source of supply.

FARMSHOP

STEAK & EGGS

SERVES 2

125 g (4½ oz) honey
2 bunches flat-leaf parsley
20 g (¾ oz) mint
20 g (¾ oz) fresh oregano
185 ml (6 fl oz/¾ cup) freshly squeezed orange juice
250 g (9 oz) carrots
3 or 4 long-stem artichokes
1 garlic clove, crushed
Olive oil
1 pinch thyme
A few black olives
Pulp of 1 lemon
2 underblade steaks
Peppercorn mix (page 260)
4 fried eggs (page 262)
1 pinch ras el hanout

Bring the honey to the boil with one bunch of the parsley, the mint and oregano tied up in a piece of muslin (cheesecloth). Add 185 ml (6 fl oz/¾ cup) water, the orange juice and carrots, sliced thinly lengthways. Mix and bring to the boil. Wait for the carrots to soften, about 5 minutes. Remove the carrots and keep reducing the liquid, stirring (about 15 minutes). Remove the outer fibres of the artichoke stems, and the leaves from the top until you reach the heart. Cut into four lengthways. Cook the crushed garlic for 3 minutes in a frying pan on a medium heat with 1 tablespoon olive oil. Add the thyme and artichoke quarters, and cook for 5 minutes. Coat the carrots in the reduced glaze and add them to the artichokes with some black olives and the pulp of the lemon, mixed with the remaining chopped bunch of parsley and drizzled with a little olive oil. Cook, stirring, for 3 minutes. Season. Season the steaks with some peppercorn mix and a pinch of salt and cook on a very high heat for 30 seconds on each side, then for about 1½ minutes on each side and another 30 seconds again on each side for a rare steak. For medium, add 1 minute on each side; for well done, 2 minutes on each side. Cut the steaks in half and serve with the sautéed vegetables and two fried eggs. Finish with a pinch of ras el hanout.

19TH ST SANTA MONICA & COLORADO

HARA SUSHI INC
TANGO MAKI ROLL
ARNOLD PALMER

DRY CLEAN EXPRESS. SANTA MONICA BLVD & BROCKTON AVE

SERVES 2

TANGO MAKI ROLL
100 g (3½ oz) Vinegared sushi rice (page 261)
2 sheets nori seaweed
1 avocado, sliced very thinly
1 mango, sliced very thinly
4 Tempura prawns (page 261)
UNAGI SAUCE
125 ml (4 fl oz/½ cup) mirin
125 ml (4 fl oz/½ cup) soy sauce
100 g (3½ oz) sugar
1 tablespoon soft brown sugar
1 carrot, sliced into rounds
1 onion, sliced into rounds
1 daikon (white radish), sliced into rounds
10 g (¼ oz) fresh ginger

ARNOLD PALMER
A legendary drink named after the golfer
whose nickname in the 1950s was The King.

TANGO MAKI ROLL
For the unagi sauce: place all of the sauce ingredients in a
saucepan and bring to the boil. Keep stirring on a low heat until
the texture is thick. Filter through a fine strainer. To assemble the
roll: spread the vinegared rice on one of the nori sheets, placed
on a sushi mat covered with plastic wrap on both sides. Place
the other sheet on top, a little above the rice. Make a line of
avocado and mango slices across the full width of the nori sheet
(reserving four slices of avocado and four slices of mango), 3 cm
(1¼ inches) high and 8 mm (⅜ inch) thick. Arrange the prawns two
by two, with the tails poking a little outside the sheet of nori on
both sides. Roll up with the help of the mat. Cut into four maki and
place a thin sliver of avocado and mango on top of each. Serve with
the unagi sauce.

ARNOLD PALMER
Pour 150 ml (5 fl oz) Home-made lemonade (see page 262) over
ice cubes, then 150 ml (5 fl oz) iced tea.

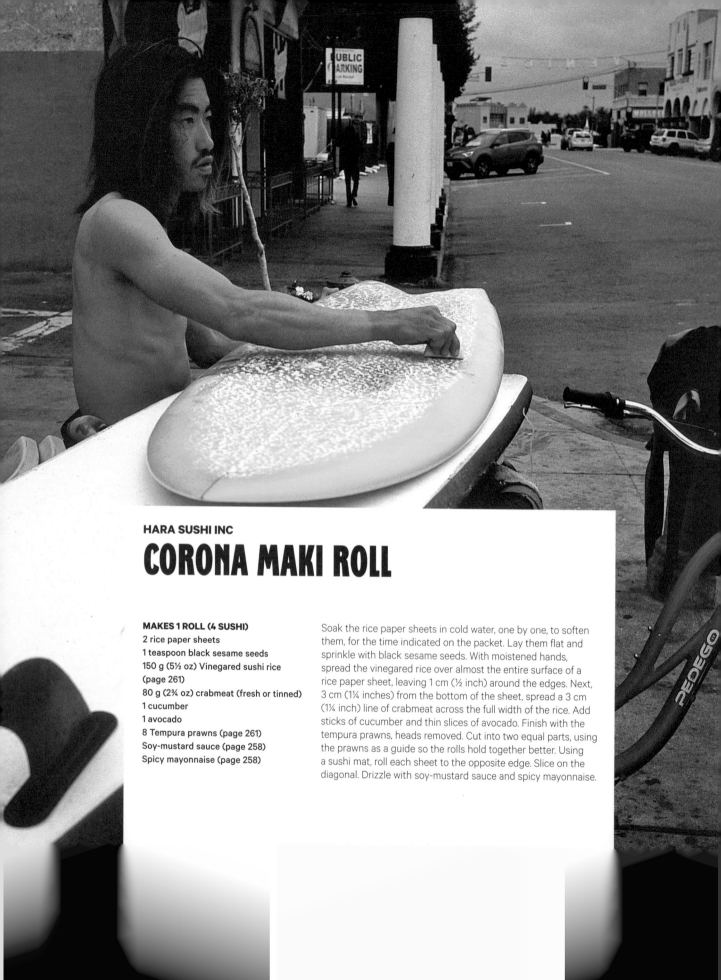

HARA SUSHI INC

CORONA MAKI ROLL

MAKES 1 ROLL (4 SUSHI)

2 rice paper sheets
1 teaspoon black sesame seeds
150 g (5½ oz) Vinegared sushi rice
(page 261)
80 g (2¾ oz) crabmeat (fresh or tinned)
1 cucumber
1 avocado
8 Tempura prawns (page 261)
Soy-mustard sauce (page 258)
Spicy mayonnaise (page 258)

Soak the rice paper sheets in cold water, one by one, to soften them, for the time indicated on the packet. Lay them flat and sprinkle with black sesame seeds. With moistened hands, spread the vinegared rice over almost the entire surface of a rice paper sheet, leaving 1 cm (½ inch) around the edges. Next, 3 cm (1¼ inches) from the bottom of the sheet, spread a 3 cm (1¼ inch) line of crabmeat across the full width of the rice. Add sticks of cucumber and thin slices of avocado. Finish with the tempura prawns, heads removed. Cut into two equal parts, using the prawns as a guide so the rolls hold together better. Using a sushi mat, roll each sheet to the opposite edge. Slice on the diagonal. Drizzle with soy-mustard sauce and spicy mayonnaise.

HARA SUSHI INC

SAKE BOMB

MAKES 1 GLASS
1 small glass heated sake
2 chopsticks
1 cold beer

Sit the glass of sake on the two chopsticks, resting parallel to each other on top of the glass of beer. Bang your fist on the table to make the sake drop down and drink in one go, shouting: 'Kanpai!'.

Located at the foot the Santa Monica apartment where I lived in 2010, every birthday, end of semester, etc. was celebrated at Hara Sushi Inc. It was always a feast. It is where I discovered the madness of Californian sushi, made from all kinds of unexpected fruit, vegetables and sauces.

S MUIRFIELD ROAD & WILSHIRE BLVD

MELROSE AVE & VINE ST

Chap. 2

DOWNTOWN LA CHINATOWN UNIVERSITY PARK ART DISTRICT

SPRINKLES CUPCAKES

VANILLA CUPCAKES

MAKES 25 CUPCAKES
VANILLA CAKE BASE
300 g (10½ oz/2 cups) soft (cake) flour
or plain (all-purpose) flour
320 g (11¼ oz) caster (superfine) sugar
12 g (¼ oz) bicarbonate of soda (baking
soda)
135 ml (4½ fl oz) milk
2 eggs
4 egg yolks
3 drops natural vanilla extract
180 g (6½ oz) butter
FROSTING
1½ egg whites
85 g (3 oz) caster (superfine) sugar
170 g (6 oz) butter
2 drops natural vanilla extract

For the cake base: mix together the flour, sugar, bicarbonate of soda and ¼ teaspoon salt. Separately, mix together the milk, eggs, yolks and vanilla. Put the dry mixture, cubed butter and half the wet mixture into the bowl of an electric standmixer. Beat on high speed for 4 minutes. Add the rest of the wet mixture in three stages, beating for 2 minutes at medium speed after each addition. Bake in muffin tins at 170°C (325°F) for 16 minutes. For the frosting: heat the egg whites and sugar in the top of a double boiler until the sugar dissolves. The mixture should be hot to the touch. Whisk with a beater to make a meringue. Add the cubed butter, ½ pinch salt and the vanilla and continue beating until light and creamy. Use a piping (icing) bag to ice the cakes.

It was in front of Sprinkles in February 2010 that I witnessed a stampede outside a restaurant for the first time. Candace, the founder, can claim to have opened the world's first cupcake bakery in Beverly Hills. Her fresh cupcakes are inimitable. This is the cupcake recipe from Blend, developed with Camilla Malmquist, a talented American pastry chef based in Paris.

NZ SINNERS. N LARCHMONT BLVD & ROSEWOOD AVE

CALIFORNIA PIZZA KITCHEN
THAI CHICKEN PIZZA

MAKES 1 PIZZA
1 large skinless chicken breast fillet
Olive oil
Thai sauce (page 257)
Pizza dough for 1 base (recipe page 262)
225 g (8 oz) grated mozzarella cheese
4 spring onions (scallions)
75 g (2½ oz) carrots
50 g (1¾ oz) bean sprouts
2 tablespoons peanuts
2 coriander (cilantro) sprigs

Flatten the chicken breast with a rolling pin, drizzle with olive oil, and season with a pinch of salt and freshly ground black pepper. In a hot frying pan brushed with olive oil, cook the chicken on a medium heat for about 2 minutes on one side. Lower the heat, turn over the breast and cook for 7–8 minutes on the other side. Dice the chicken and add to a bowl containing half the Thai sauce. Mix well. Cool, then place in the refrigerator. Spread out the dough on a floured baking tray to about 30 cm (12 inches) in diameter. Spread the rest of the Thai sauce over the base using the underside of a ladle, starting from the middle and tracing a spiral outwards. Scatter with the mozzarella cheese. In an oven heated to its maximum temperature (ideally on a pizza stone), bake for 12–15 minutes, or until the edges are golden brown. Top the cooled pizza with the diced marinated chicken and drizzle with the Thai sauce marinade left in the bowl. Bake for 5 minutes Add the thinly sliced spring onions, julienned carrots, bean sprouts, crushed peanuts and coriander.

For me, this pizza is an emblem of the Los Angeles food scene and of California, generally. All the cultures combine their inspirations and techniques in this dish, using local ingredients. This is a reinterpretation of a Thai dish as a pizza, where a peanut sauce replaces the famous tomato sauce base.

AVOCADO TOAST

MAKES 4 TOASTS
1 bunch chives
120 g (4¼ oz) ricotta cheese
1 teaspoon lemon juice
2 avocados
4 slices artisan-style bread
½ pinch paprika
½ pinch cumin
1 bulb spring onion (scallion)

Mix the chopped chives with the ricotta. Add a pinch of salt and 5 pinches freshly ground black pepper, mix, then add the lemon juice and mix again. Roughly mash the avocados. Spread the toasted bread with the ricotta-chive mix and cover the whole surface with avocado. Sprinkle with the paprika, cumin, chopped bulb spring onion and a little salt and pepper.

Bringing together generosity and finesse, DTLA CHEESE, the Grand Central Market cheese shop with a thousand different products elevates what, everywhere else would be a side-dish, to the level of a main meal. Their secret is perhaps that each item on their menu is taken very seriously. If you are not a fan of avocado, you must go there for their grilled cheese.

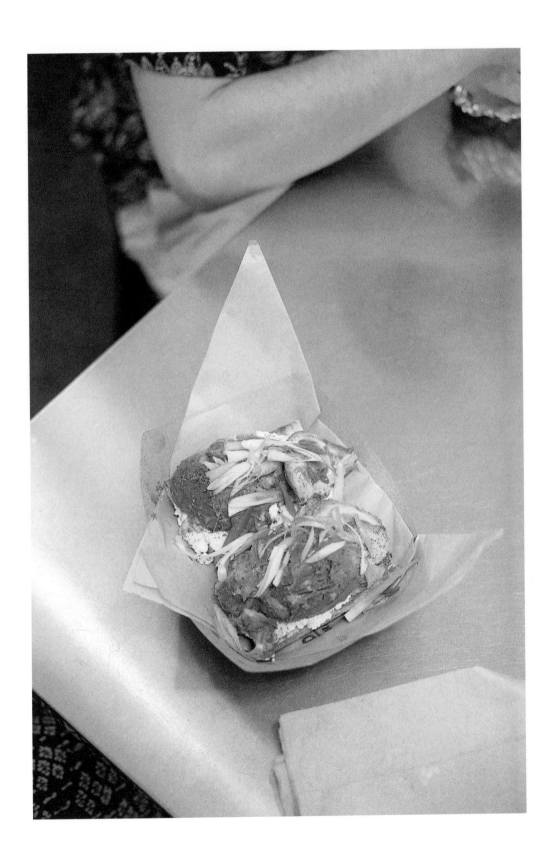

VITALITY SMOOTHIE

MAKES 1 JUICE
1 apple
200 g (7 oz) pineapple flesh
2 kale leaves
1 handful English spinach
½ avocado
½ cucumber
1 piece fresh ginger

Seed and quarter the apple and place with the rest of the ingredients in a blender. Blend for 3 minutes. The texture should be smooth and homogenous.

A customer who bought his vitality smoothie at Press Brothers Juicery very kindly made sure I did not fall from the stool I stood on to take the picture of the queue at Eggslut. Kindness and taking care of others are in the DNA of this business, created by two brothers raised on juiced fruits and vegetables, describing their mother as 'an avid juicer of 20 years'.

BACON & EGG SANDWICH

MAKES 4 MUFFINS

6 eggs

30 g (1 oz) butter

1 bunch chives

4 English muffins or brioche buns

60 g (2¼ oz) Chipotle aïoli (page 258)

4 rashers bacon

4 cheddar cheese slices

Break the eggs into a frying pan on a medium heat and add the diced butter. Stir to break the yolks. Season after 2 minutes with salt and freshly ground black pepper. Stop cooking after 5 minutes. Add the chopped chives and stir. To assemble: spread the inside of the muffin with chipotle aïoli, add the scrambled eggs topped with a rasher of bacon – fried for 5 minutes each side in a frying pan on a medium heat – a slice of cheddar, and close the muffins.

After more than an hour of waiting and almost falling off a stool, I found that Eggslut deserves this obsession. I didn't have the patience to take a photo of my sandwich. Muriel, Whitney and their friend agreed to let me hold them back a few minutes so I could immortalise theirs. Starting with unbeatable raw materials (including fresh buns), Eggslut sets itself apart with its egg-cooking know-how. It is with great humility therefore that I have created this interpretation of their dish. Obviously, the waiting time at Eggslut makes their sandwiches taste even better.

HAWTHORN AVE & HIGHLAND AVE

DUKE'S, LOS FLORES CANYON RD, MALIBU

AVOCADO-PESTO-RICOTTA TOAST CHIA SEED PUDDING

SERVES 4

AVOCADO-PESTO-RICOTTA TOAST
4 slices wholemeal (whole-wheat) bread
100 g (3½ oz) ricotta cheese
Lemon zest
2 avocados
WALNUT PESTO
1 garlic clove
50 g (1¾ oz/½ cup) walnuts
45 g (1½ oz) basil leaves
75 ml (2¼ fl oz) olive oil
2 pinches salt
50 g (1¾ oz) finely grated parmesan cheese
CHIA SEED PUDDING
450 ml (16 fl oz) coconut milk
60 ml (2 fl oz/¼ cup) agave syrup
2 pinches cinnamon
2 ripe bananas
45 g (1½ oz) chia seeds (organic food stores)
25 g (1 oz/¼ cup) desiccated coconut

AVOCADO-PESTO-RICOTTA TOAST

For the walnut pesto: crush the garlic and process with the rest of the pesto ingredients, except the parmesan, in a food processor for about 20 seconds until the texture is smooth. Add the parmesan and process for 10 seconds. For the avocado-pesto-ricotta toast: spread the toasted bread with the walnut pesto, add the ricotta, sprinkle with lemon zest and season with salt and freshly ground black pepper. Place half an avocado, sliced into rounds, on top.

CHIA SEED PUDDING

Blend together the coconut milk, agave syrup, cinnamon, a pinch of salt and one mashed banana in a food processor for about 20 seconds. The texture should be smooth. Add the chia seeds and mix. Chill for about 2 hours. Before serving, add some rounds of fresh banana and a little desiccated coconut.

Impresso Cafe felt like an oasis in the middle of downtown Los Angeles. You need to drink something slightly sour with these sweet, mild dishes, such as a kombucha tea. The coffee range is impressive here – this place is a local institution.

FRUTA CON CHILE Y LIMÓN

MAKES 1 CUP
Your choice of fruit or vegetable
Lime juice
Chilli powder

Cut up the fruit or vegetable and place it in a bowl. Pour over the lime juice and sprinkle with salt and chilli powder.

Whatever fruits or vegetables you choose, the important thing is the three secret ingredients that the holders of these stands add to give the fruits their kick. They go up and down the sidewalks at Los Angeles' major intersections as soon as the sun comes up. This recipe works with all fruits and vegetables, but the best sellers are cucumber, melon, pineapple, mango and coconut.

S HILL ST & W 3RD ST

FRENCH DIP SANDWICH

MAKES 4 SANDWICHES

1 beef stock cube
1 onion
1 carrot
1 celery stalk
1 leek
2 garlic cloves
A few thyme sprigs
900 g (2 lb) piece roasting beef
¼ teaspoon oregano
¼ teaspoon nutmeg
¼ teaspoon sage
½ teaspoon cloves
½ teaspoon allspice
4 halved baguettes or 4 buns
90 g (3¼ oz) mustard
A few large pickles (gherkins)

Preheat the oven to 150°C (300°F). Make up the beef stock with the stock cube, according to the amount of water indicated on the packet. Chop the onion and slice the carrot, celery and white part of the leek into rounds, then mix with the chopped garlic and thyme in a large baking dish. Cover the beef with all the dried herbs and spices, season well with salt and freshly ground black pepper and roast in the oven for 45 minutes, fat side up. Take the beef out of the oven, wrap it in foil and let it rest for 30 minutes. Pour the contents of the baking dish into a frying pan and cook on a high heat, stirring, until all the liquid has evaporated. Transfer to a saucepan with 480 ml (16½ fl oz) beef stock, bring to the boil on a medium heat, then reduce the heat to low. Cook for about 30 more minutes, stirring, or until half the liquid has evaporated. Strain the sauce and add a pinch of salt and pepper. Keep warm. Heat the halved baguettes in a 180°C (350°F) oven for about 3 minutes. Just before filling the sandwich, wet the cut side of the bread with the sauce, a little or a lot, and lay thin slices of roast beef on top. Serve with the mustard and the pickles, cut into quarters lengthways, on the side.

At Philippe's, the story goes that a police officer in a hurry saw his pastrami sandwich accidentally dropped into the meat juices from cooking. The next day at lunchtime, his co-workers came back and asked for the same thing at the counter. 'The rest is legend', as the staff at Philippe's like to say. Following on in the tradition of this happy accident, you can still indicate whether you want your sandwich just moistened, double-dipped or completely soaked when you order. This gives the customers a warm feeling of personalised service, despite its international success and the hundreds of sandwiches sold each day.

BANANA CREAM PIE

MAKES 1 PIE

PASTRY
150 g (5½ oz/1 cup) plain (all-purpose) flour
½ teaspoon caster (superfine) sugar
80 g (2¾ oz) butter
60 ml (2 fl oz/¼ cup) iced water

FILLING
200 g (7 oz) caster (superfine) sugar
40 g (1½ oz/⅓ cup) cornflour (cornstarch)
735 ml (25 fl oz) milk
4 egg yolks
½ teaspoon natural vanilla extract
40 g (1½ oz) butter
2½ ripe bananas

CHANTILLY CREAM
230 g (8½ oz) thin (pouring/whipping) cream, cold
2 teaspoons icing (confectioners') sugar
1 teaspoon natural vanilla extract

For the pastry: mix together the flour, ½ teaspoon salt, the sugar and cubed butter. Add the iced water, little by little, and mix; the texture should be smooth and not sticky. Shape into a ball. Roll the dough out between two sheets of baking paper. Set aside in the refrigerator for at least 1 hour (ideally 24 hours), with the baking paper. Place the pastry in a cake tin, fold the overhang inwards and press the pastry against the inside of the tin with a fork. Cover with foil, place a weight on the foil to stop it puffing up and bake at 200°C (400°F) for 20 minutes. Remove the foil and cook for 5–10 minutes more to lightly brown. For the filling: mix together the sugar, cornflour, ½ teaspoon salt and the milk. Cook on a medium heat for about 7 minutes or until bubbles appear. Reduce the heat to low and cook for a further 2 minutes. Off the heat, gradually mix in the whisked yolks. Return to a medium heat and, when it comes to the boil, cook for another 2 minutes, making sure not to scramble the eggs. Remove from the heat, stir in the vanilla and the butter in cubes, mix and let it stand. Spread half of the filling on the cooled pastry, top with some slices of banana, then make another layer of filling. Chill for 2 hours, ideally overnight. For the chantilly cream: beat the cream for 2 minutes, add the sugar and vanilla. Beat for another 2 minutes. Spread on top of the filling.

JACKS N JOE

SOUTHERN CALIFORNIA PANCAKES

MAKES 10 PANCAKES

2 eggs
200 ml (7 fl oz) milk
250 g (9 oz/1⅔ cups) plain (all-purpose) flour
175 g (6 oz) caster (superfine) sugar
1 sachet (11 g/¼ oz) baking powder
1 tablespoon icing (confectioners') sugar
120 g (4¼ oz) crème fraîche
Melted butter
A few strawberries
1 small handful blueberries
Whipped cream, to serve

Mix together the eggs and milk and, separately, mix together the flour, sugar, baking powder and a pinch of salt. Combine the two mixtures and mix until smooth. Put this batter in the refrigerator for 1 hour. Whisk the icing sugar and crème fraîche in a chilled mixing bowl until peaks form. For one pancake, pour a ladleful of batter into a non-stick frying pan brushed with melted butter. Cook for 2 minutes, or until bubbles appear. Turn and cook for two-thirds of the time the first side was cooked. Serve with sliced rounds of strawberry, blueberries and whipped cream.

Whatever the hour of day, when you go to Jacks N Joe all the staff give off the same positive energy and lightness that's essential to a successful breakfast. It's as if Jacks N Joe is protecting customers from bad news, emails and phone calls, one pancake at a time.

INTELLIGENTSIA COFFEE

ICED COFFEE

SERVES 2
350 g (12 oz) ice cubes
100 ml (3½ fl oz) full-cream (whole) milk
15 ml (½ fl oz) agave syrup
4 espresso coffees

Place a handful of ice cubes, the milk, agave syrup and the espressos in a cocktail shaker. Shake vigorously for 2–3 minutes. Strain into two glasses filled with the remaining ice cubes. Drink through a straw.

Intelligentsia Coffee is the pioneer of the 'third wave of coffee', which strives to improve every process of coffee production. Whenever I go into one of their coffee bars, I experience a religious feeling at the sight of the architecture and the staff concentrating on operating the complex machinery. Here, everything is organised around celebrating and refining the 'black gold'.

LOS ANGELES TRADE TECHNICAL COLLEGE. RALPH T. GUTHRIE SIGN PAINTING CLASS

SIGN PAINTING, RICH LESSONS FROM THE MASTER

Having always been fascinated by the art of writing in all its forms, I was familiar with the legendary Ralph 'Doc' Guthrie from his books on sign painting, as well as through videos. His talent has made him famous around the world and, when Roxanne, his assistant, confirmed that Doc would let me attend one of his classes, I was ecstatic. Doc teaches at the Los Angeles Trade Technical College, which offers the oldest sign graphics program in the United States (since 1923). I had heard about his teaching abilities, but I didn't expect to meet someone who invested as much energy on a daily basis in helping young people (or not-so-young, and some in rehabilitation) face working life in the best possible conditions, with the odds on

their side. It doesn't matter how much time or energy they need, they don't leave the college without being equipped to live their passion. This despite a tough, heavy curriculum, and students of all stripes at very different levels. I took away a very strong message of hope from Doc Guthrie. We barely had time to talk about him, he was always showing me some wonder that one of his students had already produced, relative to their level. Doc has a gift for giving students self-confidence, which is even rarer than all the other qualities for which he is known.

AVOCADO & RADISH TOAST

MAKES 3 PIECES OF TOAST
3 slices artisan-style bread
Unsalted butter
SMASHED AVOCADO
2 avocados
2 teaspoons lemon juice
1 tablespoon finely chopped onion
Salt and freshly ground black pepper
RADISH SALAD
1 handful radishes
1 tablespoon lemon juice
2 teaspoons olive oil
½ teaspoon salt
½ teaspoon freshly ground black pepper
GARNISH
Fresh dill
Fresh chives
Freshly ground black pepper
Fine sea salt
Cherry tomatoes (optional)
Slices of lemon (optional)

Roughly mash the avocados and add the rest of the smashed avocado ingredients. Mix well. Cut the radishes into matchsticks, then mix together all of the salad ingredients. Toast the bread. Cool the toast and assemble, in this order: a layer of butter, the radish salad (spread it out with your fingers right to the edge of the toast), then the smashed avocado. Sprinkle with dill, chives, pepper and fine sea salt. Garnish with cherry tomatoes and lemon slices, if desired.

Welcoming me at the entrance to the Zinc Cafe, John was the first to tell me about Alice Waters, the mother of the Californian cuisine movement and one of its strongest inspirations. Not only is it Zinc Cafe's ambition to offer dishes all day (and every day restart from scratch, since everything is home-made, from the pastries to the juices, all the dishes, pizzas, desserts and cocktails), but also to offer a constantly changing range of decorative objects and books. It was the humility of owner, John, however, that made the biggest impression on me. He follows the seasons for his menu, just as he did on the first day, greets customers with a smile, just as he did on the first day, and the dishes are still like home cooking, as they were created by either himself or his mother.

ZINC CAFE & MARKET & BAR

ASPARAGUS SANDWICH

MAKES 4 PIECES OF TOAST
400 g (14 oz) green asparagus
Olive oil
Coarse salt
60 g (2¼ oz) Japanese (panko)
breadcrumbs
30 g (1 oz) butter
300 g (10½ oz) cauliflower
50 g (1¾ oz) onion
2 garlic cloves
125 ml (4 fl oz/½ cup) thin (pouring/
whipping) cream
1 pinch ground nutmeg
4 slices artisan-style bread
100 g (3½ oz/1 cup) grated cheddar cheese
4 eggs
Vinegar

Brush the asparagus with olive oil and add 2 pinches of coarse salt. Place the asparagus on a baking tray and bake in a 220°C (425°F) oven for 12 minutes. After 6 minutes, spread out the Japanese breadcrumbs on another tray and season with coarse salt and add a few tiny pieces of the butter. Remove the leaves and stem from the cauliflower and slice the florets. Mix with the finely chopped onion and garlic, cream, nutmeg, salt, the remaining butter and 1 large pinch freshly ground black pepper. Cook this mixture with some coarse salt on a medium heat until soft. Purée the cooled mixture. Toast the slices of bread and spread them with a generous layer of cauliflower purée, add a few asparagus spears and sprinkle with cheddar. Poach the eggs in unsalted boiling water with some vinegar added for about 3 minutes. Place them on the pieces of toast. Sprinkle with breadcrumbs. Reheat in the oven for 3–5 minutes.

PALMETTO ST & MOLINO ST

MAC & CHEESE PIZZA

MAKES 4 PIZZAS

Pizza dough for 1 base (recipe page 262 or buy from your local pizzeria)

100 g (3½ oz) grated mozzarella cheese

MAC & CHEESE

115 g (4 oz) small elbow macaroni

15 g (½ oz) butter

225 ml (7¾ fl oz) full-cream (whole) milk

60 g (2 oz/¼ cup) ricotta cheese

90 g (3¼ oz) vintage cheddar cheese, grated

125 g (4½ oz) aged parmesan cheese, grated

Preheat the oven to 180°C (350°F). For the mac and cheese: cook the pasta following the packet directions. Drain. Add the butter, milk, ricotta, 70 g (2½ oz) of the cheddar, 90 g (3 oz) of the parmesan, a pinch of salt and some freshly ground black pepper to the hot pasta. Mix together quickly. Bake the pasta sprinkled with the rest of the cheddar and parmesan for 25–30 minutes, until the top is golden brown. Flatten the pizza dough on a floured surface: starting from the middle and leaving a thick edge around the outside, stretch the dough to 30 cm (12 inches) in diameter. Add the mozzarella cheese and bake in the oven at the maximum temperature setting (ideally on a pizza stone) for 15–20 minutes until the edges are brown and the mozzarella is melted. When the pizza comes out of the oven, wait 5 minutes, then spread over some mac and cheese. Return to the oven for no more than 2 minutes before serving.

The founders of Pizzannista! have shown the self-discipline required of professional skateboarders to leave a mark on their generation with their gourmet pizzeria concept. Every Sunday night, they offer what is undeniably one of the most decadent and addictive pizzas I've ever eaten: the mac & cheese pizza. Great names in skating from all over the world can be found here.

STEF. VENICE BEACH RECREATION CENTER

HERMOSA BEACH
INGLEWOOD
HUNTINGTON PARK

PARADISE BOWLS
STRAWBERRY SMOOTHIE

MAKES 1 SMOOTHIE
200 ml (7 fl oz) almond milk
1 frozen banana
1 tablespoon peanut butter
A big handful of strawberries

Blend all the ingredients together in a food processor for 2 minutes, until the mixture is smooth and creamy.

Bowl by bowl, based on the fresh produce of the day, Paradise Bowls helps make Hermosa Beach even more idyllic than it already is. It's a landmark for the locals. That day, the staff invited me to the other side of the counter with the same smile and energy they welcomed me with when I walked into their store.

CHRISTIAN. BELVEDERE SKATEPARK

ACAI BREAKFAST BOWL

SERVES 1

1 small handful goji berries
125 ml (4 fl oz/½ cup) apple juice
2 tablespoons acai powder (organic food stores)
1 frozen banana
60 g (2¼ oz) frozen blueberries
60 g (2¼ oz) frozen strawberries
1 mango
1 kiwi fruit
A few fresh blueberries

Soak the goji berries in the apple juice for 5 minutes, then take them out and set aside. Blend the apple juice with the acai powder and frozen fruit in a food processor for 30 seconds, until there are no more lumps. Serve with pieces of mango and kiwi fruit, the blueberries and the goji berries.

«LOVE FOR PIE», 13TH ST & HERMOSA AVE, HERMOSA BEACH

ETHAN

ABIGAILE
WAFFLES WITH FRIED CHICKEN

MAKES 2 SANDWICHES
CHICKEN
25 g (1 oz) soft brown sugar
40 g (1½ oz) salt
2 chicken thighs, on the bone
500 ml (17 fl oz/2 cups) buttermilk
5 g (⅛ oz) freshly ground black pepper
1 pinch cumin
1 pinch paprika
COATING
250 g (9 oz/1⅔ cups) plain (all-purpose) flour
2 teaspoons cornflour (cornstarch)
WAFFLES
Vegetable oil
150 g (5½ oz/1 cup) plain (all-purpose) flour
1 teaspoon caster (superfine) sugar
1 teaspoon baking powder
¼ teaspoon espelette pepper (gourmet
delicatessens)
50 g (1¾ oz) butter
2 large eggs, separated
240 ml (8 fl oz) buttermilk
MAPLE SYRUP BUTTER
50 g (1¾ oz) butter, softened
50 g (1¾ oz) lightly salted butter, softened
45 ml (1½ fl oz) maple syrup
1 pinch fine sea salt
Pistachio nut kernels
Apricot jam

For the chicken: dissolve the brown sugar and salt in 2 litres (70 fl oz/8 cups) water. Remove the bones and skin from the thighs and submerge them in this brining liquid overnight. Rinse them well the next day. Mix together the buttermilk, 2 teaspoons of the salt, the pepper, cumin and paprika. For the coating: mix together the flour, cornflour and season with ½ teaspoon salt and some pepper. Dip the thighs into the buttermilk mixture, then into the flour mixture. Deep-fry the chicken at 180°C (350°F) in a deep-fryer for 5–7 minutes; the crust should be golden. Alternatively, heat 4 cm (1½ inches) oil in a frying pan on a high heat and cook for 15 minutes, turning every 2 minutes. Place the fried chicken on a metal drainer or rack. For the waffles: heat a waffle maker, brushed with vegetable oil. Mix together the flour, caster (superfine) sugar, baking powder and espelette pepper. Separately, mix together the melted cubes of butter with the egg yolks and buttermilk. Gradually pour the wet mixture into the flour mixture, and mix together. Beat the egg whites to firm peaks and add them to the mixture. Mix well. Cook the waffles according to the instructions for the waffle maker. For the maple butter: whisk together the cubed, softened butters and the maple syrup, sprinkle with fine sea salt and chill. To assemble: cut the waffle in half, arrange the fried chicken on the plate and drizzle with some maple syrup and roughly crushed pistachio nut kernels. Serve with the maple syrup butter and apricot jam on the side.

Near my table at Abigaile, a large family had come together to celebrate the graduation of one of its younger members. Abigaile is that kind of place: large enough to feel comfortable and, despite a very modern menu, able to offer each generation something to their taste, because it is delicious. When you go as a group, there is another advantage, apart from being able to enjoy their novel dishes, and that is being able to share and sample them all.

OCEAN DRIVE & MANHATTAN BEACH BLVD, MANHATTAN BEACH

97 / HERMOSA BEACH

ABIGAILE

FRIED CHICKEN SANDWICH

MAKES 2 SANDWICHES

2 small potatoes

2 eggs

Harissa hollandaise (page 259)

Rocket (arugula), halved cherry
tomatoes, sliced radishes and shaved
parmesan cheese, to serve

MAPLE SYRUP-SAGE BISCUITS

5 or 6 sage leaves

500 g (1 lb 2 oz/3⅓ cups) plain
(all-purpose) flour

2 sachets (10 g/¼ oz each) baking
powder

125 g (4½ oz) salted butter, at room
temperature

115 ml (3¾ fl oz) milk

4 tablespoons maple syrup

Coarse salt

CHICKEN, MARINADE AND COATING

25 g (1 oz) soft brown sugar

2 chicken thighs

500 ml (17 fl oz/2 cups) buttermilk

1 pinch cumin

1 pinch paprika

225 g (8 oz/1½ cups) plain (all-purpose)
flour

2 teaspoons cornflour (cornstarch)

For the biscuits: finely shred, then chop the sage. Mix with the
flour, baking powder and cubed butter. Add the milk, little by little,
until it forms a slightly sticky ball. Spread the dough over a baking
tray and cut it into 12 squares. Top each biscuit with some maple
syrup and a pinch of coarse salt. Cook for 10 minutes in a 200°C
(400°F) oven. For the chicken: dissolve the sugar and 30 g (1 oz)
salt in 2 litres (70 fl oz/8 cups) water. Remove the bones and skin
of the thighs and submerge them in the brining liquid overnight.
Rinse the next day. Mix together the buttermilk, 1 teaspoon salt,
1 teaspoon freshly ground black pepper, the cumin and paprika.
Prepare the coating by mixing together the flour, cornflour,
¾ teaspoon salt and ½ teaspoon pepper. Dip the chicken into
the buttermilk mixture, then into the flour mixture. Deep-fry the
chicken at 180°C (350°F) in a deep-fryer for 5–7 minutes; until
the outside is golden. (Or heat 4 cm/1½ inches oil in a frying pan
on a high heat and cook the thighs for 15 minutes, turning every
2 minutes. Drain the excess oil.) For the potatoes: cut the
potatoes into matchsticks, rinse and drain. Heat 5 cm (2 inches)
oil to 180°C (350°F) in a frying pan on a medium heat. Gradually
add the julienned potatoes, stirring with a metal spatula. Cook
for about 4 minutes, until golden brown. Place on a baking tray
lined with paper towel. Wait for 3 minutes, then transfer them to
a mixing bowl. Season. Fry two eggs. Assemble, in this order: a
maple syrup-sage biscuit, 1 fried chicken thigh and 1 fried egg
balanced on top. Top with some harissa hollandaise and cover
with the straw potatoes. Add some rocket, halved cherry
tomatoes, sliced radish and shavings of parmesan cheese.

MANHATTAN BEACH PIER

PANN'S RESTAURANT

CHICKEN WINGS HASH BROWN

SERVES 2

About 10 chicken wings

200 g (7 oz/1⅓ cups) plain (all-purpose) flour

2 litres (70 fl oz/8 cups) peanut oil

2 potatoes

50 g (1¾ oz) salted butter

Coat the chicken wings well with the flour and deep-fry them for 8–10 minutes at 180°C (350°F), or in 5 cm (2 inches) peanut oil in a deep saucepan for 9 minutes on a high heat. Cut the potatoes into matchsticks, rinse them until the water runs clear, and drain well. In a small heavy-based saucepan, melt the butter on a low heat, without stirring. Shake the saucepan and skim any white particles from the surface. Pour the butter into a deep frying pan on a high heat to a depth of about 5 mm (¼ inch). Add the potatoes, mix and cook for 4–6 minutes on each side, making sure they don't burn. Serve the chicken wings and hash brown separately with some hot sauce and fruit.

FRENCH TOAST

SERVES 5

1 vanilla bean, split and seeds scraped
250 ml (9 fl oz/1 cup) milk
10 slices brioche
100 g (3½ oz) butter
Icing (confectioners') sugar
500 ml (17 fl oz/2 cups) thin (pouring/
whipping) cream, chilled
Maple syrup, to serve

Heat the vanilla seeds and milk in a saucepan over medium heat, but do not let it come to the boil or foam. Soak the brioche in the milk. Cook the slices in a buttered frying pan on a medium heat for about 2 minutes on one side, or until browned. Sprinkle with icing sugar before turning the brioche over. Cook on the second side for 3 minutes, or until crispy. Sprinkle with icing sugar before turning over and serving. Whip the chilled cream. (For a sweet whipped cream, add some icing sugar when the cream starts to thicken.) Serve the French toast with butter, maple syrup and cream.

If it was just about it being one of the oldest operating diners in Los Angeles, or being famous since a long scene from Pulp Fiction was filmed there, the parking lot at Pann's would not be as jam-packed as it is every day. Not only are all of its breakfasts mouthwatering, but the welcome from the staff means you always feel good when you eat there. I was very grateful to their chef Patrick, who is French, for letting me sit alongside him on several occasions.

PANN'S RESTAURANT
EGGS BENEDICT

SERVES 4

500 g (1 lb 2 oz) beef brisket
Barbecue sauce (page 257)
1 large handful English spinach
Iced water
Lightly salted butter
4 potatoes (bintje or monalisa)
Peanut or other oil for deep-frying
4 English muffins
1 large tomato
4 Poached eggs (page 262)
Hollandaise sauce (page 257)
100 g (3½ oz) cheddar cheese
100 g (3½ oz) sour cream
1 spring onion (scallion)

Bake the brisket overnight at 100°C (200°F) in an oiled baking dish, covered with foil. The next day, slice the meat across the grain very thinly, then across the slices into matchsticks. Mix the shredded meat with half of its volume of barbecue sauce. Add the spinach, stems removed, to a saucepan of boiling water with 5 teaspoons of salt. When the water comes back to the boil, take the spinach out and plunge it immediately into iced water. Drain. Sauté the spinach for 5 minutes in a frying pan on a medium heat with a small knob of lightly salted butter. Season with salt and freshly ground black pepper. Boil the potatoes for 5 minutes, cut them in half and scoop out the middle, leaving about 5 mm (¼ inch) potato inside the skin. Deep-fry the potato shells in peanut oil for 4–7 minutes at 180°C (350°F). On a halved and toasted muffin, place a slice of tomato with a pinch of salt and 1 poached egg, drizzle with hollandaise sauce and sprinkle with grated cheddar. Serve with two potato halves, the shredded beef in barbecue sauce, the sour cream, the remaining grated cheddar cheese and the chopped spring onion.

RANDY'S DONUTS
VANILLA DONUTS

MAKES ABOUT 18 DONUTS
540 g (1 lb 3 oz) plain (all-purpose) flour
20 g (¾ oz) fresh yeast (from bakery)
150 g (5½ oz/1¼ cups) icing (confectioners')
sugar
20 g (¾ oz) salt
Peanut oil
GLAZE
150 g (5½ oz) icing (confectioners') sugar
3–4 tablespoons milk or water
2 teaspoons natural vanilla extract (optional)

For the glaze: put the sugar in a bowl and stir in the water and vanilla gradually, until the sugar has dissolved and you have a smooth, pourable glaze. For the donuts: knead the flour with 215 ml (7½ fl oz) water, the yeast, icing sugar and salt in an electric stand mixer on medium speed for 11 minutes. The temperature of the dough should stay between 25° and 29°C (77° and 84°F). Let the dough prove for 45 minutes to 1¼ hours. It should triple in size. On a floured work surface, roll out the dough to a thickness of 3–4 cm (1¼–1½ inches). Use a 10 cm (4 inch) cookie cutter to cut out rounds, then cut a hole in the middle of the rounds with a 3 cm (1¼ inch) cutter. Bring a saucepan of water to the boil. Heat the oven to 60°C (140°F). Turn off the oven and place the saucepan in the oven for 20 minutes. Place the donuts on a baking tray lined with baking paper and place in the oven for 35–40 minutes. When you touch the donut, your finger should leave an imprint. Rest the donuts for 3–5 minutes, then fry them in 4 cm (1½ inches) oil in a frying pan for about 2 minutes on each side. Glaze the donuts straight after frying.

Randy's Donuts is one of the most famous bakeries in the world. The world has seen its huge donut-shaped sign on-screen in blockbuster movies. The official recipe is a very well-guarded secret.

DOUBLE CHEESEBURGER

SERVES 2

1 onion
Vegetable oil
300 g (10½ oz) minced (ground) beef
Fine sea salt
4 cheddar cheese slices
2 hamburger buns
Butter
Spreading sauce (page 257)
1 large pickle (gherkin)
1 oxheart tomato
A few leaves iceberg lettuce

Sauté the diced onion in a frying pan on a high heat with 2 tablespoons oil. Stir for 6 minutes. Shape the minced meat into four round patties and flatten them using the bottom of a plate protected with baking paper so they are thin and wide. Season with fine sea salt and some freshly ground black pepper. Cook the patties in a hot frying pan on a high heat for 2 minutes per side (for rare). After turning over the patties, lay two slices of cheddar in a star shape on each one. Halve the buns and toast them for 2 minutes in a hot frying pan with a little butter. To assemble: spread some spreading sauce on both buns and, on the bottom halves, place some rounds of pickle, a slice of tomato, two lettuce leaves (one on top of the other), some more spreading sauce, the first patty with cheese, the sautéed onion, the second patty with cheese and the top half of the bun.

This chain, which has not been franchised because it doesn't think that would be compatible with its passion for things done well, strives to offer ultra-fresh burgers, fries and milkshakes, all in an ultra-clean environment. I could spend hours watching the employees cut up their huge potatoes at the entrance of each restaurant. Considered the most popular food chain in the world, In-n-Out Burger is also known for its 'hidden menu' that lets you order sometimes decadent burgers or fries. My interpretation of their secret double cheeseburger, called a 'Double-Double, Animal Style', is still a million miles away from their own inimitable version.

W MANCHESTER BLVD & HINDRY AVE, INGLEWOOD

Chap. 4

HOLLYWOOD
BEVERLY
FAIRFAX
STUDIO CITY
BURBANK

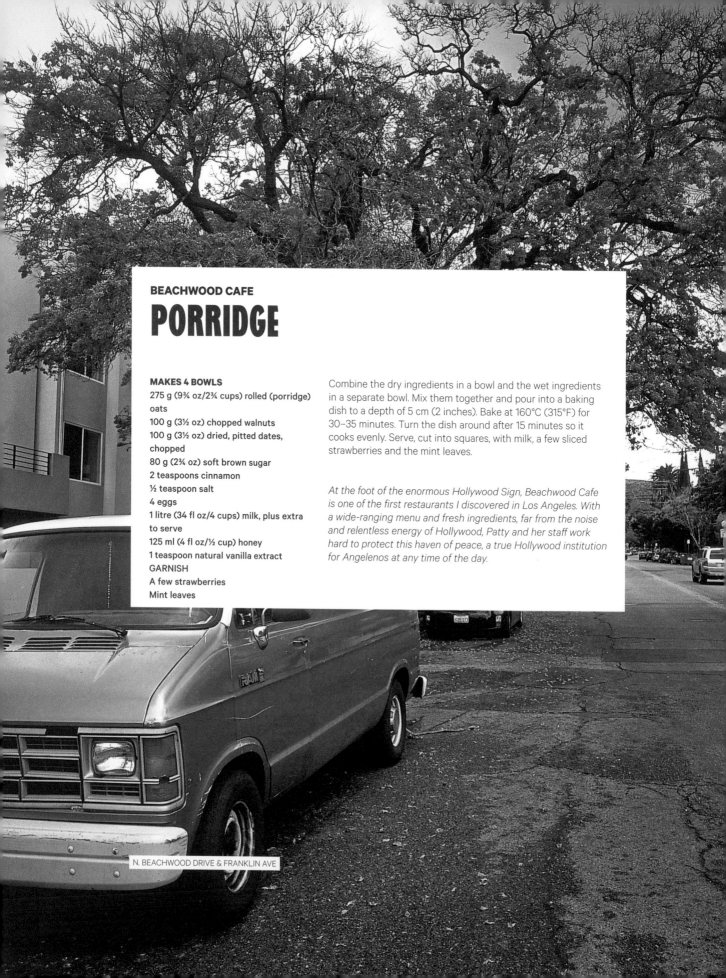

BEACHWOOD CAFE

PORRIDGE

MAKES 4 BOWLS

275 g (9¾ oz/2¾ cups) rolled (porridge) oats

100 g (3½ oz) chopped walnuts

100 g (3½ oz) dried, pitted dates, chopped

80 g (2¾ oz) soft brown sugar

2 teaspoons cinnamon

½ teaspoon salt

4 eggs

1 litre (34 fl oz/4 cups) milk, plus extra to serve

125 ml (4 fl oz/½ cup) honey

1 teaspoon natural vanilla extract

GARNISH

A few strawberries

Mint leaves

Combine the dry ingredients in a bowl and the wet ingredients in a separate bowl. Mix them together and pour into a baking dish to a depth of 5 cm (2 inches). Bake at 160°C (315°F) for 30–35 minutes. Turn the dish around after 15 minutes so it cooks evenly. Serve, cut into squares, with milk, a few sliced strawberries and the mint leaves.

At the foot of the enormous Hollywood Sign, Beachwood Cafe is one of the first restaurants I discovered in Los Angeles. With a wide-ranging menu and fresh ingredients, far from the noise and relentless energy of Hollywood, Patty and her staff work hard to protect this haven of peace, a true Hollywood institution for Angelenos at any time of the day.

N. BEACHWOOD DRIVE & FRANKLIN AVE

BEACHWOOD CAFE
SOPHIA BOWL

MAKES 2 BOWLS
120 g (4¼ oz) tofu
160 g (5½ oz) cooked brown rice
Kale side (see page 260, made without the pomegranate)
1 small cucumber
1 tablespoon finely chopped fresh coriander (cilantro)
100 g (3½ oz) kimchi (Asian food stores)
1 tablespoon finely sliced spring onion (scallion)
Peanut sauce (see page 257)
MARINADE
220 g (7¾ oz/1 cup) soft brown sugar
125 ml (4 fl oz/½ cup) soy sauce
125 ml (4 fl oz/½ cup) sesame oil

For the marinade, dissolve the sugar in 150 ml (5 fl oz) water, then add the other marinade ingredients. Cut the tofu into pieces. Add them to the marinade and set aside in the refrigerator for 3 hours. Cook the pieces of tofu in a hot frying pan on a high heat, 2 minutes per side. In a bowl, arrange: the heated brown rice, kale side, marinated tofu, rounds of cucumber sliced in half, the coriander, kimchi and finely sliced spring onion. Top with the peanut sauce.

E HARBOR BLVD & CALIFORNIA STREET MALL, VENTURA

BEACHWOOD CAFE

COLD BREW

SERVES 6
75 g (2½ oz) ground coffee
1 litre (34 fl oz/4 cups) chilled mineral water
Ice cubes

Pour the coffee and the chilled mineral water into a jar with a lid. Mix well and leave to infuse in the refrigerator for between 12 and 24 hours. Mix well again and filter. Serve in a glass filled with ice cubes and diluted with a little water, if you would like to soften the coffee flavour even more. It goes well with milk.

A cold brew wakes you up, but more gently than coffee because it doesn't have the bitterness. It is naturally sweet and reveals subtle aromas that you can't pick up when the coffee is hot.

N BEACHWOOD DRIVE & BEACHWOOD TERRACE

BEACHWOOD CAFE

FEZ BOWL

MAKES 4 BOWLS

1 very large kale leaf
1 large carrot
160 g (5½ oz) quinoa
1 French shallot
120 g (4¼ oz) shiitake mushrooms
2 tablespoons olive oil
1 large cooked beetroot (beet), grated
Harissa (page 259)
SHALLOT YOGHURT
1 finely chopped French shallot
2 small tubs Greek-style yoghurt
1 pinch salt
Juice of 1 lemon

Remove the stem and cut up the kale leaf. Slice the carrot into rounds and cook in boiling water for 2 minutes. Add the kale and cook for another 2 minutes. Cook the quinoa as per the instructions on the packet. Cook the finely chopped shallots and chopped shiitake mushrooms in a hot frying pan with a drizzle of the olive oil for 5 minutes. Add the carrot and cooked quinoa. Season with salt and freshly ground black pepper. Add the blanched kale and mix well. For the shallot yoghurt: mix all of the ingredients together. Serve in four bowls and add the beetroot, shallot yoghurt and harissa.

SUNSET BLVD & N EL CENTRO AVE

VEGGIE BURGER & KALE SIDE

SERVES 6

25 g (1 oz) dried mushrooms
60 g (2¼ oz) linseeds (flax seeds)
160 g (5½ oz) brown rice
2 onions, finely chopped
125 g (4½ oz) fresh mushrooms
4 garlic cloves, finely chopped
20 g (¾ oz) flat-leaf parsley, chopped
1 teaspoon dried thyme
2 tablespoons oregano
60 ml (2 fl oz/¼ cup) olive oil
250 g (9 oz) walnuts
12 slices of bread or 6 buns
2 avocados
2 large oxheart tomatoes
Rocket (arugula)
Kale side (page 260), to serve

Soak the dried mushrooms in hot water with the linseeds for 20 minutes. Drain and reserve the water. Toast the rice in a deep frying pan and cook it with the water from the mushrooms and linseeds for the time indicated on the packet. Sauté the onions, mushrooms, garlic and herbs for 15 minutes in a hot frying pan brushed with oil. Season with salt and freshly ground black pepper. Roughly chop the nuts in a food processor. Mix together the rice, mushrooms and walnuts, then blend them in a food processor. The final texture should be thick and malleable. Shape this mixture into 10 cm (4 inch) wide patties weighing about 130 g (4½ oz). Pan-fry them on a medium heat with a little olive oil for 2 minutes on each side. Assemble, in order: bun, patty, a quarter of an avocado, a large slice of tomato, rocket, bun. Serve with the kale side.

FINLEY FARMS. HOLLYWOOD FARMERS MARKET

BEACHWOOD CAFE

CINNAMON ROLLS

MAKES 12 ROLLS

7 g (⅛ oz) fresh yeast
1 egg
520 g (1 lb 2½ oz) plain (all-purpose) flour
50 g (1¾ oz) caster (superfine) sugar
110 ml (3¾ fl oz) milk
35 ml (1 fl oz) almond milk
1 teaspoon orange blossom water
170 g (6 oz) butter
160 g (5½ oz) soft brown sugar
15 g (½ oz) cinnamon
Glaze (see page 104)

Dissolve the yeast in 90 ml (3 fl oz) water mixed with the egg. Mix together 500 g (1 lb 2 oz) of the flour, the caster sugar and 1 teaspoon salt. Heat the milks and orange blossom water on a low heat. Before bubbles form, add 60 g (2 oz) of the butter and melt, stirring. Let the mixture cool in a mixing bowl. Add the dissolved yeast to this mixture and mix together. Pour the cooled liquid into the flour and mix in. Knead the dough for 5 minutes on a floured work surface. Let it rest under a tea towel (dish towel) for 10 minutes. Blend the remaining flour into the remaining melted butter on a low heat and stir for 2 minutes. Add the brown sugar and cinnamon. Flatten the dough into a 3 cm (1¼ inch) rectangle. Spread with the cinnamon mixture, leaving a 3 cm (1¼ inch) margin around the edges. Roll the dough starting with the longer or shorter side, depending on what size roll you want. Pinch the edges and cut into 12 rolls. Place them on a baking tray lined with oiled baking paper up against each other, touching. Cover with a tea towel and let them rise until they have doubled in volume (about 1 hour). Bake in a 190°C (375°F) oven for about 25 minutes. Lightly swirl on the frosting.

WILSHIRE BLVD & S ARDEN BLVD

CHICKEN-CHEESE PITTA SPINACH & PINEAPPLE JUICE

CHICKEN-CHEESE PITTA
SERVES 4

1 chicken stock cube
Olive oil
1 red capsicum (pepper)
1 green capsicum (pepper)
2 onions
500 g (1 lb 2 oz) skinless chicken breast fillets
4 large corn or wheat tortillas
1 bunch basil
100 g (3½ oz/1 cup) grated cheddar cheese
100 g (3½ oz) grated mozzarella cheese

SPINACH AND PINEAPPLE JUICE
SERVES 1

500 g (1 lb 2 oz) pineapple
60 g (2¼ oz) baby English spinach
100 g (3½ oz) cos (romaine) lettuce

CHICKEN-CHEESE PITTA

Dissolve the stock cube in 2 tablespoons olive oil. Add some water and mix. Sauté the seeded capsicums and thinly sliced onions on a medium heat in a frying pan with olive oil. When they start to caramelise, deglaze with half the stock cube mixture. When all the liquid has evaporated, add the sliced chicken fillets and cook for about 5 minutes, until golden. Deglaze with the rest of the stock cube mixture. Heat the tortillas on one side in a medium frying pan brushed with olive oil for 3 minutes. Flip the tortillas and top with the chicken and vegetables. Add the basil, then cover with grated cheddar and mozzarella. Fold and cut the tortilla in half, cook on both sides until the sandwich is toasted and the cheese has fully melted, or another 3 minutes.

SPINACH AND PINEAPPLE JUICE

Alternate pieces of pineapple, baby English spinach leaves and shredded cos lettuce through a juicer.

What the photo doesn't show you is how quickly the cook works. What it shows well is how generous the food vendors at the farmers' market are with fresh vegetables and herbs, which gives the pitta an incomparable flavour.

STEVE

ANNA

THE OINKSTER
FRIED CHICKEN BURGER

MAKES 4 CHICKEN BURGERS
4 skinless chicken breast fillets,
4 buns, 4 lettuce leaves, 2 large pickles
(gherkins), Buffalo sauce (page 257) and
Ranch house sauce (page 257)
THE MARINADE
450 ml (16 fl oz) fermented milk or
buttermilk, 1 teaspoon salt, ½ teaspoon
freshly ground black pepper, ½ teaspoon
paprika, ½ teaspoon cayenne pepper
THE COATING
130 g (4½ oz) plain (all-purpose) flour,
½ teaspoon salt, ½ teaspoon freshly
ground black pepper, ½ teaspoon
paprika, ½ teaspoon cayenne pepper,
1 teaspoon garlic, peanut or sunflower
oil for deep-frying

For the marinade: mix together all the ingredients and pour them into a freezer bag or mixing bowl. Add the chicken and mix to coat with the marinade. Marinate for 4–12 hours. For the coating: mix together all the ingredients in a bowl. Remove the chicken from the plastic bag and cover the chicken in the coating mixture, pressing it on firmly. Dip the chicken again in the marinade, then again in the coating. Cook the chicken in a deep-fryer at 180°C (350°F) for about 5 minutes, or in a frying pan on a medium heat with 2 cm (¾ inch) oil for 4 minutes per side. Assemble the burgers in this order: bottom half of the bun, lettuce, rounds of pickle, the fried chicken brushed with buffalo sauce, the top bun spread with the ranch house sauce.

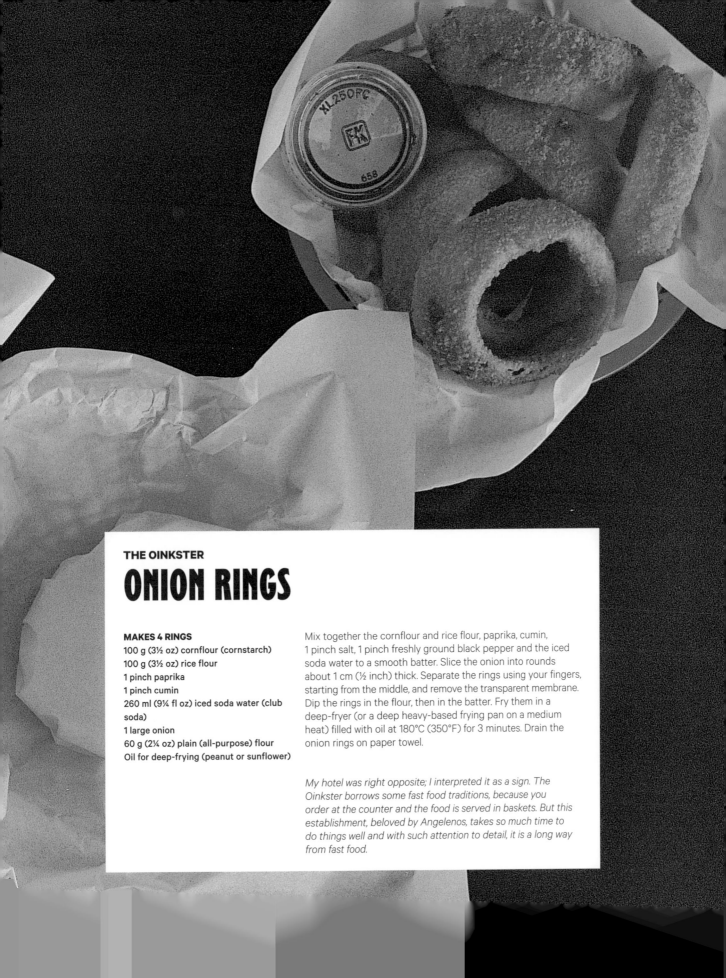

THE OINKSTER

ONION RINGS

MAKES 4 RINGS
100 g (3½ oz) cornflour (cornstarch)
100 g (3½ oz) rice flour
1 pinch paprika
1 pinch cumin
260 ml (9¼ fl oz) iced soda water (club soda)
1 large onion
60 g (2¼ oz) plain (all-purpose) flour
Oil for deep-frying (peanut or sunflower)

Mix together the cornflour and rice flour, paprika, cumin, 1 pinch salt, 1 pinch freshly ground black pepper and the iced soda water to a smooth batter. Slice the onion into rounds about 1 cm (½ inch) thick. Separate the rings using your fingers, starting from the middle, and remove the transparent membrane. Dip the rings in the flour, then in the batter. Fry them in a deep-fryer (or a deep heavy-based frying pan on a medium heat) filled with oil at 180°C (350°F) for 3 minutes. Drain the onion rings on paper towel.

My hotel was right opposite; I interpreted it as a sign. The Oinkster borrows some fast food traditions, because you order at the counter and the food is served in baskets. But this establishment, beloved by Angelenos, takes so much time to do things well and with such attention to detail, it is a long way from fast food.

BBQ CHICKEN PIZZA

MAKES 1 PIZZA

1 skinless chicken breast fillet
Oil
75 g (2½ oz) Barbecue sauce (page 257)
Pizza dough for 1 base (recipe page 262 or buy from your local pizzeria)
Smoky tomato sauce (page 258)
75 g (2½ oz) grated mozzarella cheese
BLUE CHEESE CREAM
60 g (2¼ oz) light crème fraîche (or light sour cream)
150 g (5½ oz) Bleu d'Auvergne blue cheese
100 g (3½ oz) mayonnaise
½ teaspoon Worcestershire sauce
¼ teaspoon wholegrain mustard
¼ teaspoon garlic
¼ teaspoon salt
¼ teaspoon lime juice
¼ teaspoon freshly ground pepper

For the blue cheese cream: mix together all of the blue cheese cream ingredients, cover and refrigerate for 24 hours. Flatten the chicken breast, oil it lightly and season with salt and freshly ground black pepper. In a lightly oiled heated frying pan, on a medium heat, cook the chicken for about 2 minutes on one side, reduce the heat, turn it over and cook for another 7–8 minutes. Cut the cooked chicken in half and submerge it in the barbecue sauce. Cool and place in the refrigerator. Flatten the pizza dough: starting from the middle, and leaving a thick edge around the outside, stretch the base to the size you want (about 30 cm/ 12 inches in diameter). Spread with the smoky tomato sauce using the bottom of a ladle, starting from the middle and tracing a spiral outwards. Scatter over the mozzarella cheese. Cook the pizza for between 12 and 15 minutes in an oven heated to its highest temperature (ideally on a pizza stone). Take the pizza out of the oven, cool it for 5 minutes and spread with the barbecue sauce. Add pieces of marinated chicken and drizzle with the blue cheese cream. Just before serving, bake again for no more than 2 minutes.

This place is triply legendary. It is right in the middle of the Hollywood Walk of Fame. It serves some of the best pizza by the slice in Los Angeles, for Angelenos who are homesick for NYC. Finally, its menu offers this dish that symbolises Californian cuisine: pizza with chicken and barbecue sauce.

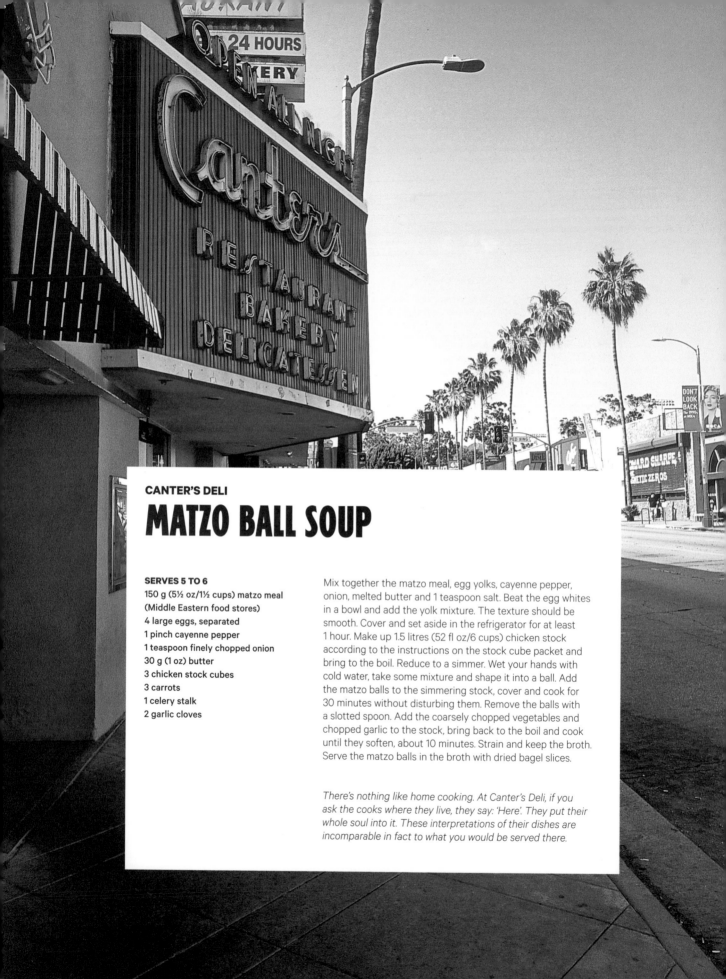

CANTER'S DELI
MATZO BALL SOUP

SERVES 5 TO 6

150 g (5½ oz/1½ cups) matzo meal
(Middle Eastern food stores)
4 large eggs, separated
1 pinch cayenne pepper
1 teaspoon finely chopped onion
30 g (1 oz) butter
3 chicken stock cubes
3 carrots
1 celery stalk
2 garlic cloves

Mix together the matzo meal, egg yolks, cayenne pepper, onion, melted butter and 1 teaspoon salt. Beat the egg whites in a bowl and add the yolk mixture. The texture should be smooth. Cover and set aside in the refrigerator for at least 1 hour. Make up 1.5 litres (52 fl oz/6 cups) chicken stock according to the instructions on the stock cube packet and bring to the boil. Reduce to a simmer. Wet your hands with cold water, take some mixture and shape it into a ball. Add the matzo balls to the simmering stock, cover and cook for 30 minutes without disturbing them. Remove the balls with a slotted spoon. Add the coarsely chopped vegetables and chopped garlic to the stock, bring back to the boil and cook until they soften, about 10 minutes. Strain and keep the broth. Serve the matzo balls in the broth with dried bagel slices.

There's nothing like home cooking. At Canter's Deli, if you ask the cooks where they live, they say: 'Here'. They put their whole soul into it. These interpretations of their dishes are incomparable in fact to what you would be served there.

CANTER'S DELI
CORNED BEEF REUBEN SANDWICH

MAKES 4 SANDWICHES
1 beef stock cube
400 g (14 oz) Corned beef (page 262)
8 slices rye bread
Russian sauce (page 257)
150 g (5½ oz) sauerkraut (fresh or tinned)
4 slices gruyère cheese
French fries, to serve
4 large pickles (gherkins), to serve

Make up the beef stock with the amount of water indicated on the stock cube packet. Cook the corned beef in the simmering broth for 3 hours. For the sandwich: spread both sides of the toasted rye bread with Russian sauce, stack with paper-thin slices of cooled corned beef, a quarter of the sauerkraut and a slice of gruyère cheese. Top with the other still-warm piece of toast. Cut the sandwiches in half and serve with fries and pickles quartered lengthways.

At Canter's, the focus is on the plate, not on the cash registers. Their corned beef, each layer of which has been scientifically tested, is a good example. Again, this is a very humble interpretation that should make you want to taste the original version, full of know-how and well-kept secrets.

FRIED CHICKEN SANDWICH & SPICY STRAWBERRY JAM

MAKES 2 SANDWICHES

Peanut or other oil for frying
2 fried eggs
2 cheddar cheese slices

SPICY STRAWBERRY JAM

130 g (4½ oz) caster (superfine) sugar
1 lemon
250 g (9 oz) strawberries
1 or 2 red chillies

BISCUIT BUNS

500 g (1 lb 2 oz/3⅓ cups) plain
(all-purpose) flour
125 g (4½ oz) salted butter
2 sachets (10 g/¼ oz each) baking powder
155 ml (5 fl oz) milk

CHICKEN

25 g (1 oz) soft brown sugar
2 boneless skinless chicken thighs
125 ml (4 fl oz/½ cup) olive oil
2 garlic cloves
1 pinch rosemary

BATTER

75 g (2½ oz/½ cup) plain (all-purpose)
flour
60 g (2¼ oz/½ cup) cornflour (cornstarch)
½ chicken stock cube
135 ml (4½ fl oz) iced soda water (club
soda)

For the strawberry jam: pour the sugar and juice and zest of the lemon over the halved strawberries. The next day, add the chillies, seeded and cut into strips of about 3 mm (⅛ inch). Bring to the boil, reduce the heat and cook for 20–25 minutes, stirring. Allow to cool. Repeat the process to obtain a jammy consistency. For the buns: gently mix together the flour, the cubed butter at room temperature and the baking powder. Add the milk, little by little, until you get a slightly sticky ball, then roll it out on a work surface to a thickness of 2 cm (¾ inch). Cut out eight biscuits with a cookie cutter (8 cm/3¼ inch diameter). Cook for 10 minutes in a 200°C (400°F) oven. For the chicken: dissolve the brown sugar and 30 g (1 oz) salt in 2 litres (70 fl oz/8 cups) water, then submerge the chicken thighs. Rinse well the next day. Mix together the olive oil, crushed garlic, rosemary and a pinch of salt and freshly ground black pepper. Coat the thighs with this marinade, cover and set aside in the refrigerator for at least 1 hour (up to 12 hours). Take the chicken out at least 30 minutes before cooking. Batter: Mix the flours with the crushed ½ chicken stock cube. Gradually pour the iced soda water into the middle and blend in. Mix until you have the consistency of a fritter batter. Dip the thighs into the batter, then fry them in the oil for 5–7 minutes in a deep-fryer at 180°C (350°F); the coating should be golden. Alternatively, heat 4 cm (1½ inches) of oil in a frying pan on a high heat and cook the thighs for 15 minutes, turning every 2 minutes. Drain off the excess oil on a rack. To assemble: open up the biscuit buns, spread both sides with the spicy jam, top with the fried chicken, a fried egg and a cheddar cheese slice. Top with the other half of the buns.

The food truck where all the film companies and studios go to grab food to feed their actors, proposed this exclusive recipe for Mother's Day. It brought back childhood memories for me, when my mother woke us up on Sunday with the smell of hot scones coming out of the oven.

PEANUT BUTTER & JELLY SANDWICH

MAKES 1 SANDWICH
2 large slices sandwich bread
40 g (1½ oz) peanut butter
40 g (1½ oz) seedless raspberry jam

Toast the bread. Spread one slice with peanut butter, the other with jam. Put the sandwich together and trim the crusts. Cut the sandwich on the diagonal.

It is a great honour to have the privilege of presenting Joan's recipes in this book, knowing that she does not like to write them down. It depends on the vegetables, the seasons, what's in the refrigerator but, most of all, what she feels like: it's a living thing! As a result, there are no written recipes at Joan's. I also had the privilege of meeting her daughters, Susie and Carol. Joan's on Third is above all a family institution.

HOLLYWOOD RECREATION CENTER. 122 COLE AVE

BACON CHILLI DOG

MAKES 1 HOT DOG
1½ rashers bacon
1 pure beef sausage
15 g (½ oz) salted butter
1 hot dog bun
80 g (2¾ oz) Chilli (see page 261)
30 g (1 oz) cheddar cheese
½ onion

Wrap the bacon around the sausage (make a cut near one end of the sausage and insert the end of the half-slice to hold it). Brush the bacon-wrapped sausage with melted butter, then pan-fry on a medium heat, rolling it so the bacon browns evenly. Place the sausage in the hot dog bun, that has been lightly warmed in the oven. Top with chilli and grated cheddar cheese and place under the grill (broiler). Once the cheese has melted, serve with diced onion.

JOAN'S ON THIRD
GRILLED CHEESE WITH TOMATO

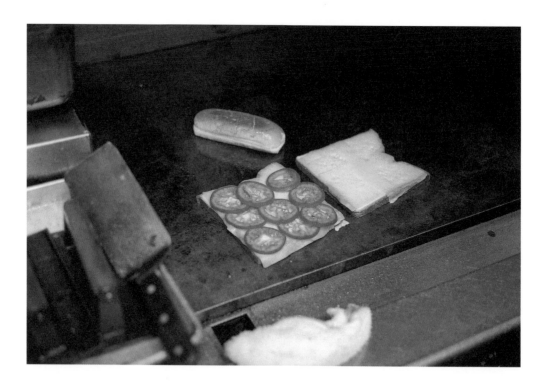

SERVES 1

50 g (1¾ oz) salted butter

2 slices sandwich bread

8 cheddar cheese slices

6–9 slices roma (plum) tomato

Lay the buttered slices of bread, butter side down, in a frying pan on a medium heat. While the bread browns, top each with four slices of the cheddar cheese. When the cheese starts to melt, arrange the tomato slices on top. After about 4 minutes, tip one slice onto the other and press down firmly with a spatula. Cut the sandwich on the diagonal when the cheese has finished melting.

PINK'S

GUACAMOLE & CHEDDAR FRIES HOT DOG

MAKES 4 HOT DOGS

1 kg (2 lb 4 oz) potatoes (bintje)
Peanut or other frying oil
8 cheddar cheese slices
Guacamole (page 260)
4 all beef sausages
4 hot dog buns
Pickled white onions (page 260)
4 large pickles (gherkins)
60 ml (2 fl oz/¼ cup) Honey mustard
sauce (page 258)

Cut the unpeeled potatoes into sticks about 5 mm (¼ inch) wide. Rinse the potato sticks until the water runs clear and leave the potatoes in the water for at least 6 hours. Drain well. Deep-fry the potatoes for 5 minutes in 140°C (285°F) oil in a deep-fryer or in 5 cm (2 inches) oil in a frying pan on a medium heat. Shake them well to drain. Cool and place in the refrigerator. At serving time, deep-fry the potatoes in 180°C (350°F) oil in a deep-fryer or in a frying pan on a high heat for 3 minutes; they should be golden brown. Drain on paper towel to remove any excess oil. Immediately add the slices of cheddar cheese and guacamole. Cook the sausage according to the instructions on the packet, or the advice of the butcher.
Heat the buns in the oven at 180°C (350°F) for 3 minutes.
To assemble: place the sausages in the buns, scatter with pickled white onions, diced pickles and honey mustard sauce.

Until there is a photo of you eating a hot dog at Pink's, you aren't officially a Hollywood star. This legendary restaurant, with its infinitely customisable hot dogs, has just celebrated its 77th birthday.

MELROSE FARMERS' MARKET
STRAWBERRY LEMONADE

MAKES 5 GLASSES
600 g (1 lb 5 oz) strawberries
30 g (1 oz) caster (superfine) sugar
100 g (3½ oz) honey
3 organic lemons

Set a few strawberries aside and cook the rest in a 180°C (350°F) oven for 10 minutes, halved and sprinkled with sugar. Once they have cooled, blend them in a food processor with the honey and 250 ml (9 fl oz/1 cup) of water for 30 seconds. Pour the mixture into a jug. Blend two unpeeled lemons with 1.25 litres (44 fl oz/5 cups) water in a food processor. (If you prefer the lemonade to be less sour, you can remove the lemon peel before blending.) Pour into the jug and add water as needed to adjust the acidity. Add a few lemon slices and strawberries to decorate and enhance the flavour of the lemonade.

When you accidentally open your analog camera thinking you have rewound your film spool, but you haven't, there is nothing like a large Mexican strawberry lemonade to lift your spirits.

BARREL & ASHES
HOT FUDGE SUNDAE

SERVES 4

12 scoops vanilla ice cream
1 handful peanuts
4 preserved cherries
HOT FUDGE SAUCE
200 ml (7 fl oz) thin (pouring/whipping)
cream
1 vanilla bean, seeds scraped
1 tablespoon icing (confectioners') sugar
160 g (5½ oz) crème fraîche
200 g (7 oz) dark chocolate
30 g (1 oz/¼ cup) unsweetened cocoa
powder
100 ml (3½ fl oz) agave syrup
50 g (1¾ oz) soft brown sugar
30 g (1 oz) salted butter

For the hot fudge sauce: whip the cream and add the vanilla bean seeds and icing sugar. Stop when the cream starts to form peaks. Bring the crème fraîche gently to the boil with the chocolate, cocoa powder, agave syrup, brown sugar, butter and a pinch of salt, stirring continuously. Turn off the heat and continue stirring for 5 minutes. Place one scoop of ice cream in the bottom of a deep glass, then a little whipped cream, a little hot fudge sauce and some roughly crushed peanuts. Repeat twice and place a preserved cherry on top.

Not least because it is made from corn, hoecake (see page 154) is now one of my five favourite dishes. Even though it is impossible for your hoecake to be as good as the one made by Michael, the chef at Barrel & Ashes, which Angelenos can't get enough of, this recipe (my interpretation) should already convince you that hoecake is not just a 'savoury pancake'.

BARREL & ASHES

HOECAKE

MAKES 3 OR 4 HOECAKES

110 g (3¾ oz/¾ cup) plain (all-purpose)
flour
100 g (3½ oz) polenta (cornmeal)
25 g (1 oz) caster (superfine) sugar
7 g (¼ oz) baking powder
5 g (⅛ oz) salt
1 egg, plus 1 extra egg white
265 ml (9½ fl oz) milk
90 g (3 oz) butter
Maple syrup
Onion rings (page 131), to serve
1 spring onion (scallion), sliced, to serve

Preheat the oven to 230°C (450°F). Mix together the dry
ingredients. Mix together one egg, one whisked egg white and
the milk. Tip the dry mixture into the wet mixture, then add
85 g (3 oz) melted butter. Blend in a food processor; the batter
should be smooth. In a hot wide ovenproof frying pan on a
medium heat, add the remaining butter in small pieces and tilt
the frying pan to spread. When it starts to foam, pour in about
a third of the batter; it must reach the edge. Cook for 2 minutes
or until bubbles form around the edges. Place the frying pan in
the oven and cook for 2–3 minutes; the centre must remain soft.
Return the frying pan to the stove on a medium heat, flip the
hoecake and cook for another 1–2 minutes; a small crust should
have formed on the underside. Pour over some maple syrup,
sprinkle with a pinch of salt and garnish with onion rings and
sliced spring onion. Serve hot.

CHILI JOHN'S
CHILLI SPAGHETTI BOWL

SERVES 8

800 g (1 lb 12 oz) thick spaghetti
480 g (1 lb 1 oz/2½ cups) dried red kidney beans
1 white onion, a few pickled green chillies (page 259) and 1 small handful soup crackers, to serve
OIL FOR THE CHILLI
2 garlic cloves
125 ml (4 fl oz/½ cup) extra-virgin olive oil
1 tablespoon chilli powder
½ teaspoon ground cumin
½ teaspoon ground coriander
½ teaspoon oregano
½ teaspoon cayenne pepper
CHILLI
1 onion
2 tablespoons canola oil
900 (2 lb) minced (ground) beef
1 teaspoon Worcestershire sauce
½ teaspoon Tabasco sauce
320 g (11¼ oz) Barbecue sauce (page 257)
1 teaspoon cayenne pepper

For the oil: sauté the chopped garlic in 1 tablespoon of the olive oil on a medium heat in a small saucepan. Stir for 2 minutes. Add the remaining olive oil and the dried spices and herbs. Heat until the oil comes to a bare simmer. Stir for about 3 minutes. For the chilli: sauté the chopped onion in the canola oil on a medium heat in a large saucepan, stirring for about 4 minutes. Add the beef and cook for about 6 minutes, stirring, or until the meat is just cooked. Add 1½ teaspoons salt, ½ teaspoon freshly ground black pepper, the Worcestershire sauce and the Tabasco sauce. Reduce the heat and add the barbecue sauce, mixing it in well. Pour all of the chilli oil into the meat, mix well. Bring to the boil on a medium heat. Reduce the heat to low and add the cayenne pepper. Cook, covered, for 15 minutes. Marinate for 3 days in a glass jar (keeps for 1 week). Cook the spaghetti according to the instructions on the packet and drain well. Reheat the beans or cook the dried beans as for chilaquiles (page 236). Serve the spaghetti, a ladleful of the chilli – having removed the excess oil – the kidney beans, some diced white onion, a few chillies in vinegar and some crackers.

Alec, Debbie and Anthony put their heart and soul into their food to keep the success of Chili John's going. It is the oldest operating restaurant in Burbank. Their recipe is hidden in a safe but, as a hint, Debbie doesn't hesitate to explain that it is a chilli in the truest Texas tradition, the recipe dating back to 1830. She adds: 'No water, no tomato, lots of salt, it's a pretty neat place'.

LARRY'S CHILI DOG

AVOCADO CHEESEBURGER

SERVES 4

3 tablespoons tomato sauce (ketchup)

½ teaspoon Tabasco sauce

4 rashers bacon

500 g (1 lb 2 oz) minced (ground) beef

8 cheddar cheese slices

4 buns

1 avocado

A few leaves of cos (romaine) lettuce

1 onion

1 tomato

1 large pickle (gherkin)

Combine the tomato and Tabasco sauces. Pan-fry the bacon on a medium heat for 5 minutes per side and drain on some paper towel. Shape the minced beef into four beef patties. Cook them on a high heat for 3 minutes on the first side. Season with salt and freshly ground black pepper. Turn them over, then lay two slices of cheddar in a star shape on each one. For a rare burger, leave it on the heat for another 3 minutes; for medium, 4 minutes; for well done, 5 minutes. Cut the buns in half horizontally and toast them. To assemble: place the cheese-topped burger on the bottom half of the bun, then two rashers of bacon, avocado slices, shredded cos lettuce, a little of the tomato-Tabasco sauce mixture, some diced onion, a round of tomato and a round of pickle. Top with the other half of the bun.

John and Veronica run one of the most respected restaurants in Burbank. No burger comes out of their kitchen without a flame over 50 cm (20 inches) high leaping up from the hotplate to give it the smoky flavour that's a signature of their restaurant.

PACIFIC COAST HIGHWAY, MALIBU

MELROSE TRADING POST

Chap. 5
VENICE
MAR VISTA

ABBOT'S PIZZA COMPANY

SALAD PIZZA

MAKES 1 PIZZA

Pizza dough for 1 base (recipe page 262, or from your local pizzeria)

2 eggs

1 small handful poppy seeds

1 small handful sesame seeds

3 or 4 garlic cloves

100 g (3½ oz) grated mozzarella cheese

½ red onion

75 g (2½ oz) light crème fraîche (or light sour cream)

1 big handful mixed salad leaves

1 tomato

½ white onion

60 g (2¼ oz) feta cheese

Lemon vinaigrette (page 259)

¼ avocado

Spread out the pizza dough to about 30 cm (12 inches) in diameter. Lightly whisk the eggs in a bowl. In another bowl, mix together the seeds and diced garlic. Brush the inside and outside edges of the pizza with the whisked eggs. Do the same with the mixed seeds – they need to stick to the egg. Sprinkle with the mozzarella and finely chopped red onion. In an oven heated to its highest temperature (ideally on a pizza stone), bake the pizza for 12–15 minutes; the edges should be golden brown. Spread a layer of light crème fraîche on the cooled pizza. Mix the salad leaves with the tomato, cut into eight wedges, the sliced half white onion and diced feta. Dress with the lemon vinaigrette. Spread the salad over the pizza. Add the avocado slices.

Whatever day of the week it is, if I go past Abbot's Pizza Company, I look at what they have ready by the slice. There is something addictive about their pizzas. I don't know if it is a secret ingredient, but it certainly has something to do with their know-how. When was I late for my classes, I appreciated their pizzas, which have the huge advantage of being able to be eaten at the wheel.

VENICE BEACH

PRAWN TACOS

MAKES 3 TACOS
3 large raw prawns (shrimp)
3 small corn tortillas
Olive oil
Baja sauce (page 257)
A few white cabbage leaves
1 sprig coriander (cilantro)
1 tomato
Tabasco sauce
3 pinches paprika
3 pinches chilli spice mix
BATTER
¼ fish stock cube
130 g (4½ oz) plain (all-purpose) flour
150 ml (5 fl oz) iced pale beer

For the batter: crush the fish stock cube in a bowl and add the flour and ½ teaspoon pepper. Gradually mix in the iced beer. Season the three peeled prawns with a pinch of salt and some freshly ground black pepper, dip them in the batter and deep-fry at 180°C (350°F) for 4 minutes. They should be crisp and golden. Drain on paper towel. Toast the tortillas for about 2 minutes on each side in a hot frying pan brushed with olive oil. For the taco, pour a little baja sauce in the middle of the tortilla, add some finely shredded cabbage, a battered prawn, some chopped coriander leaves, seedless diced tomato, some more baja sauce, some drops of Tabasco sauce, the paprika and chilli spice mix. Fold and serve.

BANH-MI CHICKEN TACO

SERVES 4

4 boneless skinless chicken thighs
1 tablespoon sugar
1½ tablespoons teriyaki sauce
250 ml (9 fl oz/1 cup) orange juice
2 garlic cloves
1 piece fresh ginger
4 tortillas
THE RADISH-CARROT PICKLE
125 ml (4 fl oz/½ cup) white vinegar
40 g (1½ oz) sugar
350 g (12 oz) radishes
220 g (7¾ oz) carrots
1 jalapeño
THE AIOLI
2 tablespoons Kewpie (Japanese)
mayonnaise
2 tablespoons hoisin sauce
2 tablespoons oyster sauce

For the pickle: bring 185 ml (5½ fl oz) water, the vinegar and sugar to the boil, mixing vigorously. Turn off the heat. Sprinkle 1 teaspoon salt over the julienned radishes and let it stand for 10 minutes. Combine the rinsed radishes with the julienned carrots and sliced jalapeño in a jar. Pour the warm pickling liquid over the vegetables and chill overnight. Clean the chicken thighs and dry them with paper towel. Mix together the sugar and 1 teaspoon each salt and freshly ground black pepper and, in a separate bowl, the teriyaki sauce, orange juice, crushed garlic and finely chopped ginger. Combine the two mixtures and add the chicken thighs. Marinate for 30 minutes to 2 hours. Cook the thighs on a low heat in a covered saucepan for 30–40 minutes, turning every 5 minutes. Turn the heat to high and cook for 3 minutes, stirring constantly. For the aïoli: whisk the Kewpie mayonnaise, hoisin sauce and oyster sauce for 2 minutes. Assemble the taco, in this order: tortilla, diced chicken topped with aïoli and pickled vegetables.

Their Vietnamese tacos are known beyond the borders. At Komodo, you can pretty much do what you like. The same goes for the staff, who don't hesitate to come to the other side of the counter to advise you or discuss. Perfect technique and understanding of the produce are shown in this brilliant concept.

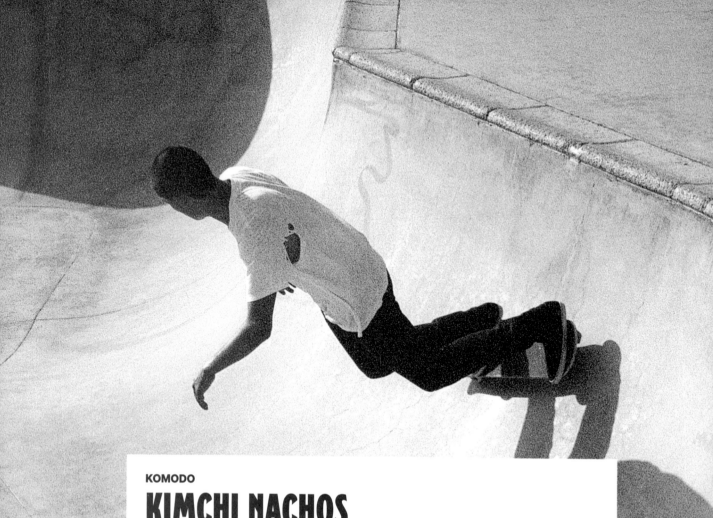

KOMODO
KIMCHI NACHOS

SERVES 2
8 corn tortillas
Peanut oil
2 tablespoons canola oil
1 tablespoon garlic
30 g (1 oz) crispy bacon
100 g (3½ oz) skinless chicken breast
fillet
225 g (8 oz) kimchi (Asian food stores)
100 g (3½ oz) tomatoes
2 tablespoons jalapeños
50 g (1¾ oz) cheddar cheese
50 g (1¾ oz) mozzarella cheese
120 g (4¼ oz) sour cream
1 spring onion (scallion)
SRIRACHA AIOLI
100 g (3½ oz) garlic cloves
85 g (3 oz) sriracha (Thai chilli sauce)
55 g (2 oz) mayonnaise

Cut the tortillas into four and deep-fry in 170°C (325°F) peanut oil until crisp and golden, or about 30 seconds. Place the corn (tortilla) chips on paper towel and season with salt and freshly ground black pepper. For the sriracha aïoli: sauté the garlic cloves on a medium heat in a frying pan for 5 minutes, stirring regularly. Blend the garlic in a food processor with the sriracha sauce and mayonnaise until the mixture is smooth. Heat the canola oil in a frying pan on the hottest heat, and add the finely chopped garlic, finely chopped bacon and diced chicken for 30 seconds. The chicken should brown. Add the chopped kimchi and the seeded and diced tomatoes and jalapeños. Cook for 30 seconds, stirring well. Season. Cook for another 30 seconds. To assemble the nachos: make a layer of corn chips, kimchi mixture and grated cheese (cheddar and mozzarella). Repeat this process three times. Sprinkle with grated cheese and bake at 190°C (375°F) until the cheese melts. Top the nachos with the sriracha aïoli, a drizzle of sour cream and a little chopped spring onion.

CHRISTIAN. BELVEDERE SKATEPARK

GREEN SMOOTHIE

MAKES 1 GLASS
150 g (5½ oz) kale
1 apple
1 banana
500 ml (17 fl oz/2 cups) almond milk

Thinly slice the kale. Cut the apple into four and remove the core. Blend all the ingredients together in a food processor and serve immediately.

I was intrigued by this pioneering company of natural detox cures, which very hotly advertises its expertise in cold-pressed juices. I discovered a team with over 12 years of expertise in the quest for wellness through food, without compromising on flavour, and their recipes are addictive. Their Downtown production facility is ultra-secure and only supplied by local farmers' markets. Thank you, Kristen!

KREATION KAFE & JUICERY

KALE JUNGLE BOWL

SERVES 1
2 kale leaves
1 small handful baby English spinach
125 ml (4 fl oz/½ cup) coconut milk
20 g (¾ oz) almond butter (organic food stores)
A few strawberries
½ banana
2 tablespoons Granola (page 196)
½ mango
80 g (2¾ oz) pineapple
A few mint leaves
Pollen (organic food stores)

Blend the kale, spinach, coconut milk and almond butter together in a food processor for about 30 seconds; the texture should be smooth and even. Pour into a large bowl and add pieces of strawberry and banana, the granola, pieces of mango and pineapple and a few mint leaves. Sprinkle with pollen.

PORCHETTA SANDWICH

MAKES 2 SANDWICHES
120 g (4¼ oz) rapini (broccoli rabe)
2 pinches chilli flakes
2 teaspoons Confit garlic (page 259)
Olive oil
200 g (7 oz) porchetta (stuffed roast pig)
1 baguette
60 g (2¼ oz) fontina cheese

Cut the rapini into pieces and mix with 3 pinches of salt, the chilli flakes, confit garlic and a tablespoon of olive oil. Let this mixture rest for 10 minutes, then spread it out on a baking tray and place under the grill (broiler) for about 3 minutes. Turn and cook for another 3 minutes. Sauté with the thinly sliced porchetta in a frying pan with a little olive oil on a high heat, stirring constantly. Cut the baguette in half and fill it with this mixture and pieces of fontina.

The fact that Travis and Kelly opened their doors to me is my greatest source of pride in this book. I had never seen such a place: Gjusta is home to one of the most well-stocked kitchens I have ever had the chance to visit. And everything is in its place. On their menu, absolutely everything is home-made under the unerring eye of Greg, a French chef who has settled in LA. In his free time, he escapes into the desert on a motorbike.

G.T.A. (GJELINA TAKE AWAY)
GUANCIALE PIZZA

MAKES 1 PIZZA

Pizza dough for 1 base (recipe page 262
or buy from your local pizzeria)
50 g (1¾ oz) grated mozzarella cheese
40 g (1½ oz) parmesan cheese
1 or 2 small green chillies
1 large handful green olives
3 thin slices guanciale (Italian food stores)
Olive oil
1 tablespoon rosemary
POMODORO SAUCE
250 g (9 oz) whole peeled tomatoes
Olive oil
½ onion
Roasted tomatoes (page 260)
½ teaspoon mixed dried herbs
½ teaspoon oregano

For the pomodoro sauce: purée the tomatoes in a blender or
food processor and add a drizzle of olive oil. Add the chopped half
onion and the roasted tomatoes and process. Bring to the boil in
a saucepan, reduce the heat to low and cook for 1 hour, stirring
regularly. Add the mixed herbs and oregano. Flatten the pizza
dough: starting from the middle, leave a thick edge around the
outside and stretch the base to the size you want (about 30 cm/
12 inches in diameter). Spread the pomodoro sauce over the base
with the bottom of a ladle, starting from the middle and tracing a
spiral outwards. Top with the mozzarella, shavings of parmesan,
round slices of chilli, the pitted and halved green olives and slices
of guanciale. Cook the pizza for 12–15 minutes in an oven heated to
its highest temperature (ideally on a pizza stone); the edges should
start to blacken. Drizzle with olive oil and sprinkle with rosemary.

G.T.A. (GJELINA TAKE AWAY)
SALMON OPEN SANDWICH

SERVES 4

250 g (9 oz) cream cheese
1 bunch chives
1 lemon
4 eggs
4 slices of artisan-style olive bread
Pickled cucumbers (page 260)
4 slices smoked salmon
1 small handful capers

Mix the cream cheese with the chopped chives (setting a few aside), the juice of the lemon and a quarter of the grated zest. Hard-boil the eggs. Spread each toasted slice of bread with the chive cream cheese, then add the pickled cucumbers, a slice of smoked salmon, and a halved hard-boiled egg. Sprinkle with a little lemon juice and half a pinch of salt and freshly ground black pepper. Sprinkle with the remaining chives and the capers.

G.T.A. (GJELINA TAKE AWAY)
EGG-KALE OPEN SANDWICH

SERVES 4

40 g (1½ oz) anchovies in olive oil
1 tablespoon wine vinegar
100 g (3½ oz) Roasted tomatoes (page 260)
Grated zest of ¼ lemon
4 handfuls kale
4 eggs
4 slices artisan-style bread
80 g (2¾ oz) provolone cheese (Italian food stores)
Olive oil

Sauté the anchovies in oil in a frying pan for 2 minutes on a medium heat, mashing them with a spatula. Deglaze the pan with the vinegar. Add the roasted tomatoes, grated zest and the well rinsed and massaged kale leaves. Cook for another 2 minutes, mixing with the spatula. Season with salt and freshly ground black pepper. Poach four eggs (see page 262). To assemble: toast the bread, place some pieces of provolone, some kale and an egg cut in half on top. Finish with a drizzle of olive oil and half a pinch of pepper.

At G.T.A. (Gjelina Take Away) the art of the open sandwich is something akin to clockmaking. That's the feeling you get when you watch the cooks preparing take-away dishes and meals.

GJUSTA

SALMON PLATE

MAKES 4 PLATES

4 eggs
8 slices smoked salmon
2 handfuls baby salad leaves and a
mixture of herbs
100 g (3½ oz) Pickled red onions (page
260)
100 g (3½ oz) Cucumber and radish
pickles (page 259)
1 handful capers
Juice of 1 lemon
Olive oil
LABNEH (YOGHURT CHEESE)
300 g (10½ oz) yoghurt

For the labneh: place the yoghurt in the middle of a piece of muslin (cheesecloth) with a pinch of salt. Fold in the edges and sit the wrapped yoghurt in a sieve over a bowl. Place in the refrigerator overnight. Hard-boil the eggs, cooking them for 6 minutes and 45 seconds. Allow to cool. To assemble: arrange all the ingredients, except the lemon juice, oil and eggs, on a plate. Top with the halved, hard-boiled eggs, dress with lemon juice, drizzle some olive oil on the labneh and season with salt and freshly ground black pepper.

ASPARAGUS & MUSHROOM FOCACCIA

MAKES 10 FOCACCIA
FOCACCIA
1 kg (2 lb 4 oz) plain (all-purpose) flour
30 g (1 oz) fresh yeast (from bakery)
20 g (¾ oz) salt
200 ml (7 fl oz) olive oil
Coarse salt
TOPPING
170 g (6 oz) oyster mushrooms
225 g (8 oz) asparagus
Olive oil
Coarse salt
55 g (2 oz) Confit garlic (page 259)
170 g (6 oz) truffle cheese (brie, pecorino or Brillat-Savarin)
140 g (5 oz) fontina (Italian cheese)
10 eggs
50 g (1¾ oz) thyme
Zest of 1 lemon

For the focaccia: knead together the flour, yeast, salt and 600 ml (21 fl oz) water until you have a smooth dough, about 10 minutes. Incorporate 50 g (1¾ oz) of the olive oil and another 50 g (1¾ oz) water. Knead for another 5 minutes. Shape into a ball. Leave the dough to prove for 1 hour at room temperature on a floured work surface. Divide the dough into 10 focaccia, and spread the dough on baking trays lined with baking paper. Brush with a mixture of 150 ml (5 fl oz) water and the remaining olive oil. Let the dough prove again for 1½ hours at room temperature. Scatter with coarse salt. For the topping: sauté the mushrooms and asparagus, brushed with olive oil and sprinkled with coarse salt, in an oiled frying pan on a medium heat. Mix together and cook for 5 minutes. Scatter the focaccia with the mushrooms and asparagus, confit garlic and thin slices of the cheeses. Break an egg on top of each focaccia and spread it out. Sprinkle with thyme and lemon zest and bake in the oven for 15 minutes at the hottest temperature setting (ideally on a pizza stone).

GJUSTA

MULTIGRAIN PORRIDGE

MAKES 2 BOWLS
50 g (1¾ oz) millet
50 g (1¾ oz/¼ cup) red quinoa
50 g (1¾ oz) farro
½ vanilla bean
½ teaspoon cinnamon
50 g (1¾ oz) steel-cut oats
160 ml (5¼ fl oz) non-dairy milk
2 apricots
A few cherries

Cook the millet, red quinoa on a low heat in about 720 ml (24½ fl oz) water. Cook the farro according to the packet directions, then add to the millet and quinoa. Add the half vanilla bean, split in two, the cinnamon and ½ pinch of salt. Cook for another 10 minutes, stirring. Add the steel-cut oats and 250 ml (9 fl oz/1 cup) water. Cook until the grains soften, about 7 minutes. Serve with milk and the fruit.

MOTOR CYCLE SWAP MEET, VETERAN'S STADIUM, LONG BEACH

VILLAGE CAR WASH, 12415 VENICE BLVD LOS ANGELES

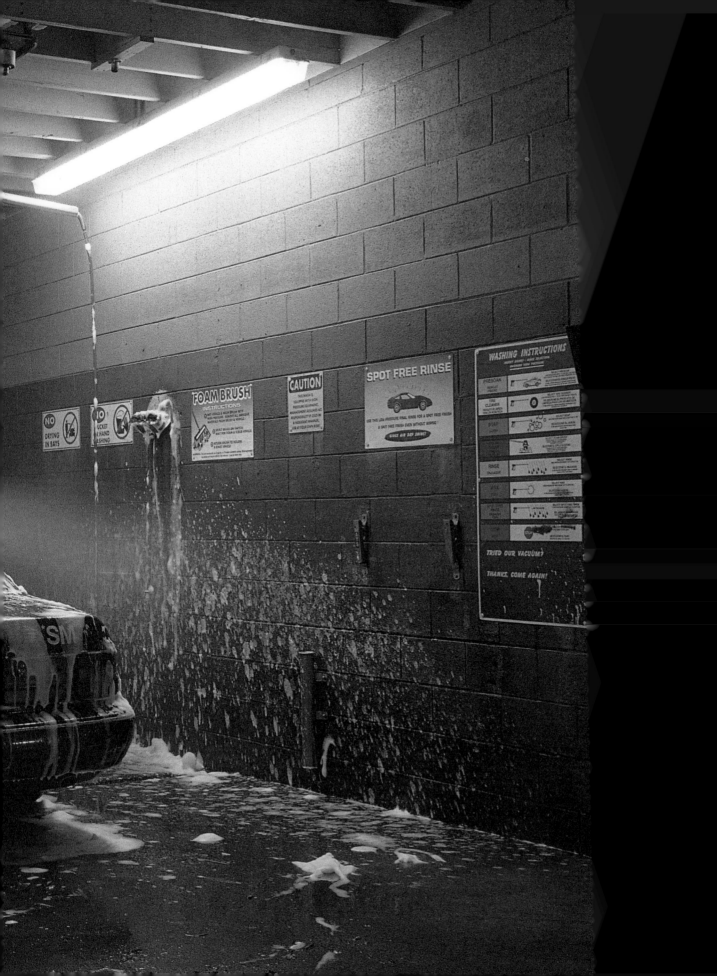

MUSHROOM BOWL

MAKES 3 BOWLS
100 g (3½ oz) brown rice
Olive oil
1 small onion
1 garlic clove
1 tomato
80 g (2¾ oz) broccoli or kale leaves
1 teaspoon Confit garlic (page 259)
1 tablespoon white wine vinegar
250 g (9 oz) mushrooms (porcini,
chanterelles or black trumpet
mushrooms)
Rosemary and fresh thyme
3 eggs
HOT SAUCE
1 tomato, peeled
30 ml (1 fl oz) hot water
1 small onion, chopped
45 ml (1½ fl oz) sriracha sauce (Thai hot
sauce)

Wash the rice three times and drain well. Lightly brown the rice in an oiled saucepan on a medium heat for about 4 minutes, stirring regularly. Blend together the onion, garlic and tomato with some salt in a food processor. Add this purée to the rice and simmer with 350 ml (12 fl oz) water. When the liquid has reduced down to the level of the rice, cover with a lid and cook for another 2 minutes. Let it rest for at least 20 minutes. Cook the chopped broccoli or kale leaves in simmering water, drain and add the confit garlic and mix. Season well with a mixture of 2 teaspoons olive oil, the vinegar, a pinch of freshly ground black pepper and pinch of salt. Sauté the mushrooms in a frying pan brushed with olive oil on a high heat for about 3 minutes, stirring. Reduce the heat to medium and add the rosemary and thyme. Cook for 5 minutes, stirring once a minute. Remove the mushrooms and, in the same frying pan, fry the eggs. Heat some olive oil, first add the white, then the yolk when the white just starts to simmer. Using a spatula, cover the yolk with the white, rotating the frying pan, to make a ball. Place the eggs on paper towel. For the hot sauce: blend the tomato with the hot water, onion, 2 pinches of salt and the sriracha sauce in a food processor. Assemble, in order: rice, mushrooms, kale and fried egg with a drizzle of hot sauce on top.

GJUSTA
GRANOLA

MAKES 1 KG (2 LB 4 OZ)

300 ml (10½ fl oz) maple syrup
75 g (2½ oz/⅓ cup) soft brown sugar
½ teaspoon cinnamon
A few drops natural vanilla extract
120 g (4¼ oz) chopped almonds
400 g (14 oz/4 cups) rolled (porridge) oats
100 g (3½ oz) pepitas (pumpkin seeds)
50 g (1¾ oz) black sesame seeds
100 g (3½ oz) sunflower seeds
2 tablespoons grapeseed oil
Almond milk, to serve
Berries, to serve

Heat the maple syrup and sugar in a pan until the sugar dissolves. When the mixture reaches about 40°C (105°F), add the cinnamon, ½ teaspoon salt and the vanilla extract. Pour over the almonds, oats and seeds and stir to coat. Spread the mixture over a baking tray brushed with grapeseed oil and cover with a sheet of baking paper. Bake at 160°C (315°F) for about 1 hour, stirring every 15 minutes. The granola should be golden brown when ready. Serve with almond milk and berries.

GJUSTA

CARROT CAKE

MAKES 1 CAKE
400 g (14 oz) caster (superfine) sugar
130 g (4½ oz) soft brown sugar
480 ml (17 fl oz) grapeseed oil
6 eggs
375 g (13 oz/2½ cups) plain (all-purpose)
flour
2½ teaspoons cinnamon
¼ teaspoon cloves
½ teaspoon nutmeg
1½ teaspoons baking powder
1¼ teaspoons bicarbonate of soda
(baking soda)
600 g (1 lb 5 oz) carrots
1 tablespoon fresh grated ginger
FROSTING
500 g (1 lb 2 oz) cream cheese
170 g (6 oz) mascarpone cheese
70 g (2½ oz) icing (confectioners') sugar
Zest of 1 lemon

Blend the sugars and the oil in a food processor until the sugars have dissolved. Add the eggs, one at a time, mix in well, then add the flour, spices, baking powder, bicarbonate of soda and ½ teaspoon salt. Blend until there are no more lumps. Add the grated carrots and ginger. Blend again; the mixture needs to be smooth. Pour into a cake tin and bake at 160°C (315°F) for 45–50 minutes. For the frosting: beat the cream cheese well for about 3 minutes. Add the mascarpone, mix, then add the sifted icing sugar. Blend in a food processor until smooth. Finish with the lemon zest and process in three or four short bursts. Cut the cooled carrot cake in half and spread half the frosting on the bottom half. Add the top layer of cake and frost the top with the remainder of the frosting.

VENICE BLVD & OAKWOOD AVE, VENICE

POKE-POKE

HAWAIIAN TUNA POKE

SERVES 1
120 g (4¼ oz) tuna fillet (sashimi quality)
3 tablespoons soy sauce
1 tablespoon sesame oil
2 pinches sesame seeds
1 green chilli
A few macadamia nuts
1 small white onion
1 spring onion (scallion)
80 g (2¾ oz) Vinegared sushi rice (page 261)

Cut the tuna into 2 cm (¾ inch) dice and mix with the soy sauce and sesame oil. Marinate in the refrigerator for 2 hours. Add the sesame seeds, the chilli sliced into rounds, the roughly crushed macadamia nuts, and the sliced white and spring onions. Place the cooled rice and tuna mixture in a bowl. This dish goes very well with diced ripe avocado, pickled ginger and wasabi.

These are the hands of Jason, a photographer, who often comes to Poke-Poke. This restaurant is located on the waterfront in Venice Beach. They were the first to offer these Hawaiian-style bowls of Ahi Tuna, and they remain the best. Jason is not the only one who thinks so!

STEVE RICHARDS. BELVEDERE SKATEPARK. EAST CESAR E CHAVEZ AVE, EAST LOS ANGELES

PLANT FOOD & WINE
VEGAN LASAGNE

SERVES 2

MACADAMIA CREAM
150 g (5½ oz) macadamia nuts
240 ml (8 fl oz) water
2 teaspoons nutritional yeast
½ teaspoon lemon juice
¼ teaspoon salt

PISTACHIO PESTO
60 g (2¼ oz) pistachio nut kernels
15 g (½ oz) English spinach leaves
40 g (1½ oz) basil leaves
4 tablespoons extra-virgin olive oil
1 teaspoon lemon juice

RED CAPSICUM MARINARA
1 tomato
½ red capsicum (pepper)
30 g (1 oz) sun-dried tomatoes
1 tablespoon French shallot
1 teaspoon lemon juice
¼ teaspoon chilli flakes
2 teaspoons olive oil

HERB-INFUSED OIL
10 g (¼ oz) English spinach leaves
5 g (⅛ oz) basil
240 ml (8 fl oz) olive oil

ZUCCHINI NOODLES AND HEIRLOOM TOMATOES
2 medium zucchini (courgettes)
Olive oil
2 oxheart tomatoes

GARNISH
Cherry tomatoes
Fresh basil

For the macadamia cream: soak the macadamia nuts in 500 ml (17 fl oz/2 cups) water for 7 hours and drain. Blend all the remaining macadamia cream ingredients together in a food processor. The final texture should be like ricotta cheese. For the pistachio pesto: process the pistachio nut kernels in short bursts, add the spinach, herbs and half a teaspoon salt and process again in short bursts. Mix in the lemon juice and olive oil. Don't overprocess, keep it the texture of a pesto. For the red capsicum marinara: seed the tomato and the half capsicum and blend with the sun-dried tomatoes (soaked beforehand in water for 4 hours and squeezed out), the shallot, lemon, ¼ teaspoon salt and the chilli flakes in a food processor, adding the olive oil, little by little, with the processor still running. For the herb-infused oil: gently process the spinach, basil, oil and a pinch of salt together in a food processor. Strain and put in a bottle. For the zucchini noodles: using a mandoline, cut 18 slices of zucchini, about 7 cm (2¾ inches) long and 2 mm (¹⁄₁₆ inch) thick, and lay them on baking paper with a little oil. Season with salt and dab the zucchini with paper towel to absorb any excess moisture. Slice the tomatoes to the same shape. To assemble: brush a plate with herb-infused olive oil and make a layer of zucchini, a layer of sauces (pesto, marinara, cream), three overlapping zucchini slices, a layer of sauces, a layer of tomatoes, three zucchini slices and finish with some pesto and macadamia cream. Garnish with cherry tomatoes and basil.

It was Nadja and Karen, whom I met the day before in Gjusta, who opened the doors of this vegan temple to me, which has an international vegan cooking school on the first floor above the restaurant. Thank you, Leigh, for your hospitality!

N CAHUENGA BLVD & LEXINGTON AVE

MOTOR CYCLE SWAP MEET, VETERAN'S STADIUM, LONG BEACH

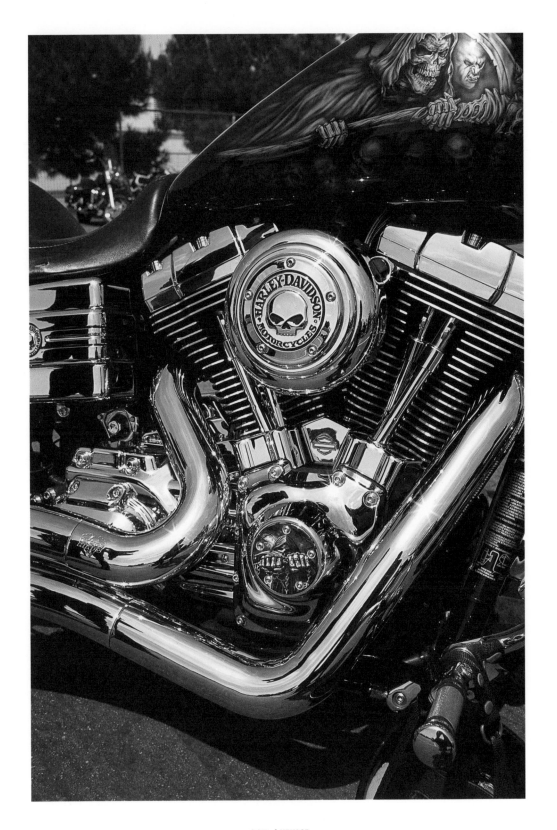

SANTOUKA (MITSUWA MARKET)
PORK RAMEN

MAKES 4 BOWLS RAMEN
Vegetable oil
300 g (10½ oz) wheat noodles, thin
2 spring onions (scallions)
A few sheets nori seaweed (dried or fresh)
THE TONKOTSU BROTH
750 g–1 kg (1 lb 10 oz–2 lb 4 oz) pork bones
(trotters or leg bones)
Spring onions (scallions) or salad onions
THE BRAISED PORK
500 g (1 lb 2 oz) pork belly
150 ml (5 fl oz) soy sauce
125 ml (4 fl oz/½ cup) sake
15 ml (½ fl oz) mirin (very mild sake)
30 ml (1 fl oz) oyster sauce
50 g (1¾ oz) sugar
3 garlic cloves, 1 French shallot, 1 onion,
1 carrot
DEGLAZING LIQUID
2 tablespoons soy sauce, 2 tablespoons mirin

For the broth: submerge the pork bones in a large quantity of water, bring to the boil and cook for 15 minutes. Take the bones out and clean the pot. Bring the same quantity of fresh water to the boil. Meanwhile, rinse the bones and remove any remaining impurities. Simmer the bones again for 20 minutes, removing any scum or solids that rise to the top. Cover and cook for at least 3 hours, ideally 10–12. Strain. For the braised pork: tie the pork into a compact shape, with the meat on the inside. Bring a saucepan of water to the boil with all the braised pork ingredients, leaving the garlic, shallot and onion unpeeled and slicing the carrot into rounds. Pour this mixture over the pork belly and bake in a 135°C (275°F) oven for at least 3 hours, turning it over every hour. The pork needs to be half-submerged in the liquid at all times. Cool the braised pork in its juices, then slice. Sauté the slices in vegetable oil on a high heat. For the deglazing liquid: mix together the soy sauce and mirin and deglaze the meat. To assemble: in a large bowl, pour in some boiling broth, the noodles, cooked according to the instructions on the packet, the deglazed pork, one or two pinches of chopped spring onion, and the nori seaweed prepared as per the instructions on the packet.

BEEF UDON

MAKES 4 BOWLS UDON

300 g (10½ oz) udon noodles

400 g (14 oz) beef, thinly sliced

1 tablespoon grapeseed oil

60 ml (2 fl oz/¼ cup) soy sauce

60 ml (2 fl oz/¼ cup) mirin (very mild sake)

2 spring onions (scallions)

60 g (2¼ oz) wakame seaweed

THE DASHI

30 g (1 oz) kombu seaweed

1 litre (35 fl oz/4 cups) mineral water

20 g (¾ oz) dried bonito flakes

For the dashi: cook the kombu in the mineral water for 2 hours (don't let the temperature rise above 70°C/158°F). Add the dried bonito and let it infuse for 3 minutes, then strain the dashi. Cook the udon noodles as per the instructions on the packet. Sauté the beef slices in oil on a very high heat until coloured. Mix together a tablespoon of the soy sauce and a tablespoon of the mirin and deglaze the pan. Add the rest of the soy sauce and mirin to the dashi, bring to the boil and reduce the heat to low. Season with salt and freshly ground black pepper. Serve the dashi soup, udon, spring onions and beef scalding hot in a bowl. Garnish with the wakame seaweed.

Each of my visits to the Mitsuwa Market Place has been unforgettable, from every mouthful of ramen or scalding hot udon that I've eaten, to just wandering through the Japanese supermarket, where you can find everything you want (fresh and in the grocery aisles). These two dishes require patience to be successful. On that front, no one can match Santouka for ramen and Sanuki for udons. Their reputation is international, and their secrets are as well kept as the formula for Coca-Cola.

VENTURA
MALIBU
PACIFIC PALISADES

MULLIGATAWNY SOUP
ROOTY FRUITY JUICE

ANOO CHANDRASHAKER'S RECIPE

MAKES 1 SOUP TO SERVE 5

115 g (4 oz) butter
5 carrots
120 g (4¼ oz) onions
4 celery stalks
2 garlic cloves
1 teaspoon turmeric
1 tablespoon curry powder
1 bay leaf
180 g (6½ oz) basmati rice
210 g (7½ oz) red lentils
2 apples
1 large potato
1 sweet potato
240 ml (8 fl oz) coconut milk

MAKES 1 JUICE

200 g (7 oz) beetroot (beet), 200 g (7 oz) apple, 200 g (7 oz) carrot,
1 piece fresh ginger

SOUP

Heat the butter in a large saucepan on a medium heat and add
the diced carrots and onions, sliced celery and crushed garlic.
Cook, stirring, for 6 minutes, until everything softens. Add the
spices, bay leaf and ½ teaspoon freshly ground black pepper, cook
for another 3 minutes. Add 2 litres (70 fl oz/8 cups) water and let
the mixture simmer for 30 minutes. Add the rice, lentils, diced
apples and potatoes. Cook for another 20 minutes, covered. Add
the coconut milk and cook, stirring, for 5 minutes. Season with
1 teaspoon salt.

JUICE

Juice all of the ingredients, alternating with pieces of ginger.

Every Wednesday morning, Steve's farm opens its doors to keen volunteers. Each day, the harvest makes it way to The Farmer and the Cook restaurant, which he runs with his wife, Olivia, in Ojai, Ventura. The whole menu of the restaurant is organised around what the farm produces. Although it is located on the site of a former prison, it is the intense feeling of freedom enjoyed by Nicolas and Johnny, Steve's employees, that I will remember. They go surfing almost every day before or after the harvest and wouldn't change their job for anything in the world.

RANCHO DEL PUEBLO FARM. RICE ROAD & BALDIUM ROAD, OJAI

STEVE'S PICK-UP TRUCK, W EL ROBLAR DR & N LA LUNA AVE, OJAI

NEPTUNE'S NET SEAFOOD RESTAURANT

FISH & CHIPS
SANGRIA

FISH AND CHIPS
SERVES 4

110 g (3¾ oz/¾ cup) plain (all-purpose) flour
1 teaspoon garlic powder
1 egg
1 fish stock cube
300 ml (10½ fl oz) cold beer
4 long cod fillets
200 g (7 oz) Japanese (panko) breadcrumbs
French fries, to serve
Tartare sauce (page 258), to serve

SANGRIA
MAKES 1 LITRE (35 FL OZ/4 CUPS)

1 apple
1 orange
A few mint leaves
30 g (1 oz) soft brown sugar, plus extra
150 ml (5 fl oz) Sprite
100 ml (3½ fl oz) Coca-Cola
750 ml (26 fl oz) red Burgundy wine
30 ml (1 fl oz) orange juice

FISH AND CHIPS

Mix together the flour, garlic powder, 1 teaspoon salt and ½ teaspoon freshly ground black pepper. Add the egg. Dissolve the fish stock cube in the cold beer and mix with the egg and flour mixture. Cut the fish fillets in half on the diagonal, dip them in the flour, then dip them in the batter and finally in the breadcrumbs, pressing them on well. Deep-fry the fillets at 180°C (350°F) for 4 minutes in a deep-fryer or for 3 minutes each side in 1 cm (½ inch) oil in a frying pan on a medium heat. Serve with French fries and the tartare sauce.

SANGRIA

Core the apple, cut it into wedges and thinly slice the wedges across. Seed and cut the orange into wedges, without peeling. Place the apple and orange into a carafe with the mint and brown sugar. Mash with a wooden spoon for about 1 minute. Add the soft drinks and mash again. Pour in the wine, mixing at the same time. Adjust the taste with more or less orange juice and brown sugar.

This is a legendary place for all bikers around the world. Located at the intersection of the famous Mulholland and Pacific Coast Highways, two major thoroughfares for Californian road trips, you enjoy some of the best fish and chips in the country under the deafening roar of Harley Davidsons – all opposite one of Malibu's most beautiful surf spots.

ZUCCHINI SPAGHETTI BOLOGNESE

SERVES 4
6 zucchini (courgettes)
Basil, to serve
BOLOGNESE SAUCE
2 garlic cloves
2 onions
1 tablespoon olive oil
1 bay leaf
200 g (7 oz) minced (ground) veal
2 tomatoes
400 ml (14 fl oz) tomato passata (puréed tomatoes)
30 g (1 oz) butter
2 tablespoons fish sauce

W CHANNEL ROAD & PACIFIC COAST HIGHWAY

For the bolognese: sauté the roughly chopped garlic and thinly sliced onions in the olive oil in a saucepan on a high heat until the onions are translucent and starting to brown. Add the bay leaf. Gradually add the minced meat on a medium heat. Season with salt and freshly ground black pepper. Add the roughly chopped tomatoes and passata on a low heat. Simmer for at least 10 minutes. At the end of the cooking time, add the butter and fish sauce. Remove the bay leaf. Julienne the zucchini and draw out the liquid with some salt. Add the zucchini to boiling water for 1 minute, drain and pat dry while still hot. Mix the zucchini with the sauce and serve with basil.

The day before I visited Caffe' Delfini, Cindy Crawford confessed to Alex and Gianpetro that they ran the most romantic restaurant in the world! When they were getting established, they accepted the challenge that California seemed to be posing them, using their Italian know-how: 'Make food that is delicious, but not fattening'. One day, by chance, at the market, Alex discovered zucchini that was cut and cooked like spaghetti. With a veal-based bolognese sauce, it became the legendary 'zinguine' of Caffe' Delfini.

CAFFE' DELFINI

ALCOHOL-FREE DECAF TIRAMISU

SERVES 6

5 eggs, separated
150 g (5½ oz/⅔ cup) caster (superfine)
sugar
500 g (1 lb 2 oz) mascarpone cheese
Mug of prepared decaffeinated coffee
2 packets ladyfinger biscuits (savoiardi)
30 g (1 oz) dark chocolate, finely grated

Whisk the egg yolks with the sugar, add the mascarpone and mix together. Beat the egg whites to soft peaks and add to the mascarpone mixture. Pour the cooled mug of decaffeinated coffee into a deep plate and roll the ladyfingers quickly in the liquid so they don't become too soggy. In a rectangular dish, arrange a layer of biscuits, then a layer of cream. Repeat the process. Dust with the grated chocolate, cover with plastic wrap and set aside in the refrigerator for 24 hours.

VENTURA PIER, VENTURA

CALIFORNIA ST MALL & VENTURA PROMENADE

Chap. 7
SILVER LAKE
WESTLAKE
HIGHLAND PARK
LOS FELIZ

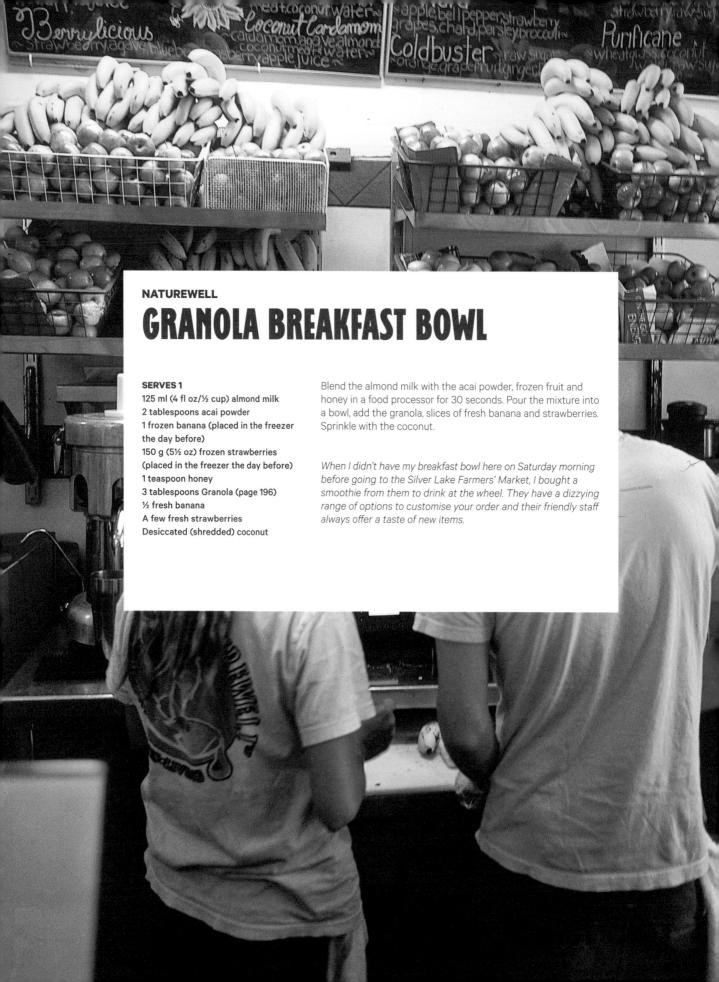

NATUREWELL

GRANOLA BREAKFAST BOWL

SERVES 1

125 ml (4 fl oz/½ cup) almond milk
2 tablespoons acai powder
1 frozen banana (placed in the freezer the day before)
150 g (5½ oz) frozen strawberries (placed in the freezer the day before)
1 teaspoon honey
3 tablespoons Granola (page 196)
½ fresh banana
A few fresh strawberries
Desiccated (shredded) coconut

Blend the almond milk with the acai powder, frozen fruit and honey in a food processor for 30 seconds. Pour the mixture into a bowl, add the granola, slices of fresh banana and strawberries. Sprinkle with the coconut.

When I didn't have my breakfast bowl here on Saturday morning before going to the Silver Lake Farmers' Market, I bought a smoothie from them to drink at the wheel. They have a dizzying range of options to customise your order and their friendly staff always offer a taste of new items.

NATUREWELL
DATE-COCONUT SMOOTHIE

MAKES 1 SMOOTHIE

3 or 4 dates

250 ml (9 fl oz/1 cup) coconut milk

60 g (2¼ oz) fresh coconut meat

1 small handful almonds

1 frozen banana

1½ tablespoons Granola (page 196)

1 teaspoon maca powder (organic food stores)

1 tablespoon hemp protein powder (organic food stores)

Pit the dates and place them with the rest of the ingredients in a blender. Blend for approximately 30 seconds or until smooth.

TACOS DELTA

TACOS AL PASTOR HORCHATA

SERVES 6 TO 8

TACOS AL PASTOR

1 kg (2 lb 4 oz) pork fillet
6–8 corn tortillas
1 tablespoon olive oil
Tabasco sauce
1 large onion
½ bunch coriander (cilantro)
4 limes
Tabasco sauce, to serve
MARINADE
1 pineapple
3 garlic cloves
½ bunch coriander (cilantro)
125 ml (4 fl oz/½ cup) orange juice
60 ml (2 fl oz/¼ cup) white vinegar
25 g (1 oz) chilli powder
1 teaspoon oregano
1 teaspoon cumin
1 teaspoon white pepper
2 small chipotle chillies in adobo sauce (sold in tins at specialty stores)
2 teaspoons adobo sauce (sold in tins at specialty stores)
2 teaspoons salt

HORCHATA

200 g (7 oz) rice
20 g (¾ oz) cinnamon, plus extra for sprinkling
400 ml (14 fl oz) sweetened condensed milk
400 ml (14 fl oz) evaporated milk
30 g (1 oz) blanched almonds
50 g (1¾ oz) caster (superfine) sugar
Ice cubes

TACOS AL PASTOR

Flatten out the pork well. For the marinade: dice half of the pineapple (put some aside) and juice the rest. Mix together the halved garlic, half a bunch of coriander and the remaining marinade ingredients in a bowl. Transfer to a bag, add the pork and make sure it is well impregnated with the marinade. Place in the refrigerator on a plate overnight. Remove the pork from the plastic bag and cook the pork and its marinade in the oven for 30 minutes at 220°C (425°F), or until it starts to brown. Take the fillet out of the oven and turn it over. Lower the oven to 180°C (350°F) and cook for 1½ hours. Cut the pork into slices or small cubes and return it to the dish with the rest of the marinade. Toast the tortillas for about 2 minutes on each side in a hot frying pan brushed with olive oil. To assemble the taco: place some marinated pork with a little Tabasco sauce on the tortilla, add some diced onion, chopped coriander and a few pieces of diced pineapple. Serve with a wedge of lime and some Tabasco sauce.

HORCHATA

Submerge the well-rinsed rice and 15 g (½ oz) of the cinnamon in about 250 ml (9 fl oz/1 cup) water in a bowl. Mix together with your fingers. Let the rice soften for at least 3 hours. Blend in a food processor at maximum speed with the condensed and evaporated milks, blanched almonds and sugar for at least 3 minutes. Transfer to large jug with 2.25 litres (70¾ fl oz) water and a little more cinnamon. Mix together. Serve with ice cubes and sprinkle with more cinnamon.

The bright colours, the sign lettering, the atmosphere, the aromas: I love everything about Tacos Delta. This is where I went to eat the best breakfast in the world: chilaquiles (see page 236). The recipe has been passed down over generations and is a well-guarded secret. So even if you try your hardest with this recipe, which is my interpretation, their original version will transport you to Mexico City, where I tasted them for the first time a few years earlier.

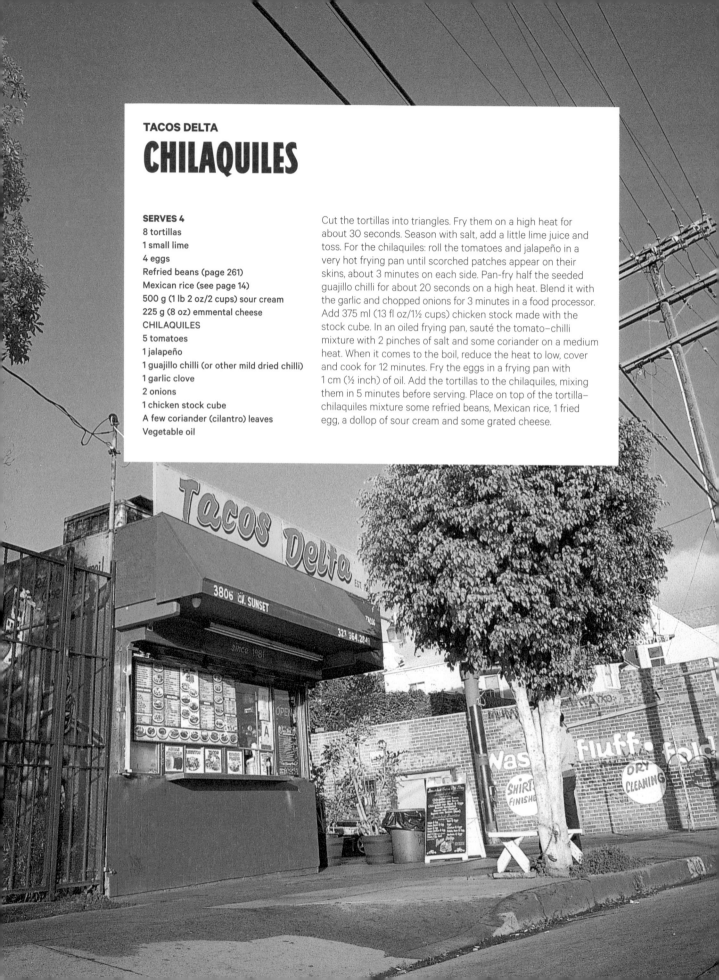

TACOS DELTA
CHILAQUILES

SERVES 4
8 tortillas
1 small lime
4 eggs
Refried beans (page 261)
Mexican rice (see page 14)
500 g (1 lb 2 oz/2 cups) sour cream
225 g (8 oz) emmental cheese
CHILAQUILES
5 tomatoes
1 jalapeño
1 guajillo chilli (or other mild dried chilli)
1 garlic clove
2 onions
1 chicken stock cube
A few coriander (cilantro) leaves
Vegetable oil

Cut the tortillas into triangles. Fry them on a high heat for about 30 seconds. Season with salt, add a little lime juice and toss. For the chilaquiles: roll the tomatoes and jalapeño in a very hot frying pan until scorched patches appear on their skins, about 3 minutes on each side. Pan-fry half the seeded guajillo chilli for about 20 seconds on a high heat. Blend it with the garlic and chopped onions for 3 minutes in a food processor. Add 375 ml (13 fl oz/1½ cups) chicken stock made with the stock cube. In an oiled frying pan, sauté the tomato–chilli mixture with 2 pinches of salt and some coriander on a medium heat. When it comes to the boil, reduce the heat to low, cover and cook for 12 minutes. Fry the eggs in a frying pan with 1 cm (½ inch) of oil. Add the tortillas to the chilaquiles, mixing them in 5 minutes before serving. Place on top of the tortilla–chilaquiles mixture some refried beans, Mexican rice, 1 fried egg, a dollop of sour cream and some grated cheese.

GLUTEN-FREE LEMON CAKE VIETNAMESE COFFEE

MAKES 1 CAKE

110 g (3¾ oz) butter, 150 g (5½ oz/⅔ cup) caster (superfine) sugar, 2 eggs, 2 lemons, 90 g (3 oz) superfine brown rice flour (organic food stores), 10 g (½ oz) tapioca flour, 35 g (1¼ oz) potato starch, 35 g (1¼ oz/⅓ cup) almond meal, ½ teaspoon xanthan gum, ½ teaspoon bicarbonate of soda (baking soda), 85 ml (2¾ fl oz) lemon juice, 85 ml (2¾ fl oz) fermented milk, ½ teaspoon natural vanilla extract
GLAZE
2 tablespoons hot water, 1 tablespoon milk, 150 g (5½ oz) icing (confectioners') sugar, 15 g (½ oz) butter, 1 small lime, 1 or 2 drops natural vanilla extract

VIETNAMESE COFFEE
SERVES 1
3 espresso coffees (25 ml/¾ fl oz each), 25 ml (¾ fl oz) sweetened condensed milk, 150 g (5½ oz) ice cubes

THE CAKE

Beat the butter and sugar in a cold bowl for 5 minutes. Add the eggs and zest of the lemons and blend in a food processor for 5 minutes; the texture should be smooth and uniform. In another bowl, mix together the flours, potato starch, almond meal, xanthan gum, bicarbonate of soda and ½ teaspoon salt. Mix the lemon juice with the fermented milk and vanilla in a glass. Combine the three mixtures. Pour the batter into a greased tin and bake at 180°C (350°C) for 45 minutes to 1 hour; the blade of a knife inserted into the cake should come out clean. For the glaze: mix the hot water and milk with the icing sugar, melted butter, lime juice and vanilla until well blended. Pour over the warm cake.

THE VIETNAMESE COFFEE

Mix the espressos and condensed milk together well. Pour over ice cubes in a glass. Serve with a straw.

Although sadly now closed, on the edge of the Silver Lake Farmers' Market, Mornings Nights Cafe was the neighbourhood café where all the locals liked to meet. As well as their delicious gluten-free cakes, you could find your caffeine fix here to get your day off to a good start.

ORIGINAL TOMMY'S
CHILLI CHEESEBURGER

MAKES 4 CHEESEBURGERS
THE CHILLI
450 g (1 lb) minced (ground) beef
1 carrot
1 beef stock cube
1 tablespoon olive oil
2 tablespoons chilli spices
½ teaspoon salt
½ teaspoon paprika
½ teaspoon garlic powder
½ teaspoon onion powder
½ teaspoon pepper
1 tablespoons cornflour (cornstarch)
1 tablespoon white vinegar
4 tablespoons plain (all-purpose) flour
1 pinch cayenne pepper

THE CHEESEBURGER
500 g (1 lb 2 oz) minced (ground) beef
Fine sea salt
8 cheddar cheese slices
4 hamburger buns (or white English muffins)
A little butter
1 onion
2 tablespoons honey mustard
1 large gherkin (pickle)
1 large oxheart tomato

For the chilli: bring the beef to the boil with 750 ml (26 fl oz/3 cups) water, the carrot and stock cube. When the water has evaporated, add the rest of the chilli ingredients. Cook on a low heat for about 2 hours. For the cheeseburger: shape the beef for the burger into four patties, season with the sea salt and cook in a hot frying pan on a high heat, 3 minutes per side for rare. Flip the burgers and lay two slices of cheddar in a star shape on each one. Halve the buns and toast for 2 minutes in a hot frying pan with a little butter. Assemble, in order: bottom half of bun, patty with melted cheese, chilli, diced onion, honey mustard, gherkin slices, slice of tomato, top half of bun.

In seventy years, few businesses can claim to have had as many imitators. At Tommy's, Angelenos eat in their car in the central parking lot or at one of the stand-up tables all around. Faithful to the wish of its founder, Tommy Koulax, they still add 1–2 ladlefuls of chilli to every item on the menu.

S WESTLAKE AVE & S ALVARADO ST

CHRISTINA. MELROSE TRADING POST

W OLYMPIC BLVD & S ALVARADO ST, LOS ANGELES

KITCHEN MOUSE
PARFAIT

MAKES 10 BOWLS GRANOLA
300 g (10½ oz/3 cups) rolled (porridge) oats
40 g (1½ oz) linseeds (flax seeds)
35 g (1¼ oz) pepitas (pumpkin seeds)
35 g (1¼ oz) sesame seeds
30 g (1 oz) sunflower seeds
40 g (1½ oz) chia seeds
½ teaspoon salt
60 ml (2 fl oz/¼ cup) brown rice syrup (organic food stores)
555 ml (19 fl oz) maple syrup
60 ml (2 fl oz/¼ cup) coconut oil
475 ml (16¾ fl oz) hot water
1 vanilla beans, seeds scraped
2 teaspoons natural vanilla extract
Yoghurt
Fresh fruit

Mix all of the dry ingredients together. Mix the rice syrup with 80 ml (2½ fl oz/⅓ cup) of the maple syrup. Mix the wet and dry mixtures together and place on a baking tray lined with baking paper and brushed with coconut oil. Bake in a 160°C (315°F) oven for about 30 minutes, stirring every 10 minutes. Pour 250 ml (9 fl oz/1 cup) of the hot water over the split vanilla bean and extract in a bowl. Stir. Pour in the rest of the water and the remaining maple syrup. Mix well and let the syrup cool. Discard pod. To make a parfait: pour about 80 g (2¾ oz) yoghurt into the bottom of the bowl, then the same volume of granola and fresh fruit. Top with 2–3 tablespoons of the vanilla–maple syrup.

Erika, the founder of Kitchen Mouse, fell in love with the space. She set up her café in because of its high ceilings that were reminiscent of New York, where she has spent half her life. What makes her huevos rancheros (see page 250) delicious is her recipe for enchilada sauce. Despite the crowds of customers on the day I visited, I was very touched by Erika's patience and generosity, while running one of the greatest restaurants in Los Angeles. It's somewhere I could easily eat every day, all year long.

KITCHEN MOUSE

GOMASIO BROWN RICE CAKES

SERVES 2

200 g (7 oz) cooked brown rice
1½ tablespoon sesame seeds
2 tablespoons Ponzu sauce (page 258)
2 tablespoons agave syrup
1 spring onion (scallion)
3 tablespoons coconut oil
80 g (2¾ oz) oyster mushrooms
Coriander chutney (page 260)
Lemon chilli sauce (page 258)
4 pinches gomasio
CHILLI AND PURPLE MIZUNA SALAD
A few small shishito or green chillies
1 tablespoon olive oil
1 large handful of purple mizuna

Process half the cooked rice in a food processor until a ball forms. Mix this ball with the rest of the cooked rice, along with the sesame seeds, ponzu sauce, agave syrup and finely chopped spring onion. Shape the mixture into small round pucks, about 2 cm (¾ inch) thick and 6 cm (2½ inches) wide. Cook these rice cakes in a frying pan with 2 tablespoons of the coconut oil for about 3 minutes on each side. Sauté the mushrooms in a frying pan on a high heat with the remaining coconut oil, stirring constantly. For the salad: brush the shishito chillies with olive oil and season with 2 pinches of salt. Cook them in a frying pan on a very high heat stirring regularly for about 5 minutes, or until they soften and their skin starts to bubble. Let them cool, then mix with the mizuna. Place two rice cakes and some coriander chutney on a plate, and top with the chilli and mizuna salad dressed with the lemon chilli sauce. Sprinkle each plate with gomasio.

HUEVOS RANCHEROS

SERVES 2

8 small corn tortillas
80 g (2¾ oz) Refried beans (page 261)
4 Fried eggs (page 262)
100 g (3½ oz/1 cup) grated cheddar cheese
A few green cabbage leaves
1 bunch coriander (cilantro)
A few pepitas (pumpkin seeds)
1 bulb spring onion (scallion)
1 avocado
1 small lime
ENCHILADA SAUCE
1 onion
60 ml (2 fl oz/¼ cup) olive oil
120 g (4¼ oz) crushed tomatoes
55 g (2 oz) tomato paste (concentrated purée)
30 g (1 oz) rice flour
35 g (1¼ oz) chilli powder
½ teaspoon garlic powder
1 teaspoon salt
½ teaspoon ground cumin
½ teaspoon oregano
1 pinch ground cloves
300 ml (10½ fl oz) orange juice
300 ml (10½ fl oz) vegetable stock
1 red chilli

For the enchilada sauce: sauté the diced onion with 1 tablespoon of the olive oil in a frying pan on a high heat, stirring, for 2 minutes. Reduce the heat to medium, then add the tomatoes, tomato paste, remaining olive oil and the rice flour. Cook for about 1 minute. Add the spices, orange juice and vegetable stock and cook for 5 minutes, until the mixture thickens. Sauté the chilli on a very high heat in a frying pan until scorched patches appear on the skin, about 3 minutes. Add the amount of chilli you like to the sauce and blend in a food processor. To assemble: cover a plate with enchilada sauce, place four hot tortillas on top, top with sauce, then add refried beans and two fried eggs. Add some more sauce, top with grated cheese and place the dish in the oven to melt the cheese. Add the chopped green cabbage, some coriander leaves, pepitas, sliced spring onion and half an avocado. Squeeze over a little lime juice.

ALCOVE CAFÉ & BAKERY

COBB SALAD

SERVES 2

3 tablespoons olive oil
2 tablespoons mustard
1 garlic clove
1 pinch dill
1 skinless chicken breast fillet (about 120 g/4¼ oz)
2 eggs
6 rashers smoked bacon
½ cos (romaine) lettuce
½ iceberg lettuce
2 tomatoes
80 g (2¾ oz) Bleu d'Auvergne blue cheese
1 ripe avocado
1 pretzel or half a baguette
Vinaigrette (page 259)

Whisk 2 tablespoons of the olive oil with the mustard for 2 minutes, then add the crushed garlic, dill, and a pinch each of salt and freshly ground black pepper; whisk for another 3 minutes. Place the chicken, cut into strips, in this marinade, cover and set aside in the refrigerator for at least 1 hour (or up to 12 hours). Cook the chicken in a hot frying pan on a medium heat with the remaining olive oil for 4 minutes on each side. Cook two hard-boiled eggs. Lay the bacon on a baking tray between two sheets of baking paper. Bake at 130°C (250°F) for 25 minutes. Place a mixture of the shredded lettuces in a deep plate, then arrange the diced seeded tomatoes, cooled diced marinated chicken, small squares of cooled bacon, cubes of blue cheese, a boiled egg and a sliced half avocado. Serve the pretzel and vinaigrette on the side.

The Cobb Salad is one of Los Angeles' most iconic dishes. With its vinaigrette and pretzel, the version at Alcove, which I always order with a chai tea, is my favourite.

ABBOT KINNEY BLVD & BROOKS AVE, VENICE

DANNY. BELVEDERE SKATEPARK

THE BASICS

SAUCES

BARBECUE SAUCE

½ onion
240 g (8¾ oz) tomato sauce (ketchup)
115 g (4 oz) soft brown sugar
5 g (⅛ oz) butter
240 ml (8 fl oz) water
50 ml (1½ fl oz) vinegar
1 tablespoon Worcestershire sauce
1 teaspoon salt
¼ teaspoon freshly ground black pepper
¼ teaspoon celery seeds

Chop the onion, mix with the rest of the ingredients in a saucepan and cook on a medium heat for 15 minutes, stirring regularly.

BAJA SAUCE

1 teaspoon coriander (cilantro)
60 g (2¼ oz/¼ cup) mayonnaise
60 g (2¼ oz) light crème fraîche or light sour cream
1 teaspoon lime juice
½ teaspoon mustard
1 pinch celery salt
½ pinch freshly ground black pepper
½ pinch cayenne pepper

Chop the coriander and mix with the rest of the ingredients. Place in the refrigerator for 1 hour.

SPREADING SAUCE

110 g (3¾ oz) mayonnaise
110 g (3¾ oz) tomato sauce (ketchup)
1 teaspoon Savora mustard sauce
2 tablespoons cornichons (baby gherkins)
½ teaspoon salt
½ teaspoon freshly ground black pepper
½ teaspoon sugar
1 teaspoon cider vinegar

Whisk together the mayonnaise, tomato sauce and Savora. Mix in the finely diced cornichons and the other ingredients. Mix vigorously for 2 minutes. The sauce should be smooth and thick.

RANCH HOUSE SAUCE

10 g (¼ oz) parsley
15 g (½ oz) parmesan cheese
1 garlic clove
180 g (6½ oz) mayonnaise
120 g (4¼ oz) buttermilk
1 pinch tarragon
1 pinch dill
1 pinch chives
1 teaspoon mustard
1 teaspoon onion powder
½ teaspoon salt
½ teaspoon freshly ground black pepper

Mix together the chopped parsley, grated parmesan cheese, crushed garlic and the rest of the ingredients. Set aside in the refrigerator for at least 30 minutes.

PEANUT SAUCE

1 garlic clove
120 g (4¼ oz) peanut butter
2 tablespoons soy sauce
1 tablespoon sesame oil
1 teaspoon soft brown sugar
1 teaspoon lemon juice
125 ml (4 fl oz/½ cup) water

Crush the garlic and blend with the rest of the ingredients in a food processor for 1 minute.

THAI SAUCE

4 garlic cloves
200 g (7 oz) peanut butter
230 ml (7¾ fl oz) hoisin sauce
60 ml (2 fl oz/¼ cup) water
4 tablespoons sesame oil
2 tablespoons wine vinegar
2 tablespoons oyster sauce (Asian food stores)
2 tablespoons honey
2 teaspoons ground ginger
2 teaspoons soy sauce
2 pinches cayenne pepper

Chop and crush the garlic and mix with the rest of the ingredients in a saucepan. Bring to the boil on a medium heat, stirring. Cook for 1 minute, then remove from the heat.

BUFFALO SAUCE

150 ml (5 fl oz) Tabasco sauce
100 g (3½ oz) butter
20 ml (½ fl oz) white vinegar
½ teaspoon Worcestershire sauce
½ teaspoon cayenne pepper
½ teaspoon garlic powder
½ teaspoon celery salt
½ teaspoon white pepper

Mix everything together and bring to the boil, stirring constantly. When the sauce comes to the boil, take off the heat but keep stirring well.

HOLLANDAISE SAUCE

200 g (7 oz) butter
4 egg yolks
15 ml (½ fl oz) lemon juice
1 teaspoon mustard
1 pinch salt
1 pinch freshly ground black pepper

Melt the butter on a low heat, without stirring. Place the egg yolks in a heavy-based saucepan. On a very low heat, whisk the eggs for at least 5 minutes; the volume must at least double without the eggs cooking. Gently incorporate the melted butter, continuing to whisk. When the sauce has doubled in volume, add the lemon and mix it in. Add the mustard, salt and pepper.

RUSSIAN SAUCE

40 g (1½ oz) mayonnaise
30 g (1 oz) light crème fraîche (or light sour cream)
25 g (1 oz) tomato sauce (ketchup)
15 ml (½ fl oz) cornichons (baby gherkins)
15 ml (½ fl oz) lemon juice
1 teaspoon horseradish
1 pinch salt
1 pinch freshly ground black pepper

Mix the mayonnaise, crème fraîche and tomato sauce together well for 3 minutes. Add the diced cornichons and the other ingredients, mix together for 3 minutes.

CAESAR SALAD SAUCE

MAKES 500 ML (17 FL OZ/2 CUPS)

45 g (1½ oz) parmesan cheese
25 ml (¾ fl oz) wine vinegar
25 ml (¾ fl oz) balsamic vinegar
¾ teaspoon Tabasco sauce
1 teaspoon Worcestershire sauce
1 tinned anchovy in oil
25 g (1 oz) mustard
25 ml (¾ fl oz) lemon juice
1 teaspoon salt
1 teaspoon freshly ground black pepper
400 g (14 oz) mayonnaise

Blend the grated parmesan cheese and the rest of the ingredients, except the mayonnaise, in a food processor. The texture should be smooth and creamy. Add the mayonnaise, whisk, and add some water if necessary.

TARTARE SAUCE

2 large gherkins (pickles)
1 tablespoon capers
120 g (4¼ oz/½ cup) mayonnaise
1 tablespoon wine vinegar
1 teaspoon mustard
1 pinch freshly ground black pepper
1 pinch salt

Mix the diced gherkins, chopped capers and the remaining ingredients in short bursts in a food processor until well mixed but not puréed.

SMOKY TOMATO SAUCE

200 g (7 oz) tomato sauce (ketchup)
130 g (4½ oz) tomato paste (concentrated purée)
15 g (½ oz) soft brown sugar
80 ml (2½ fl oz/⅓ cup) water
2 teaspoons chilli spice mix
1 teaspoon liquid smoke (American food stores)
2 tablespoons grapeseed oil

Mix all the ingredients together in a saucepan, bring to the boil and cook for 1 hour.

TAHINI SAUCE

240 g (8¾ oz) tahini (Middle Eastern or organic food stores)
470 ml (16½ fl oz) water
60 ml (2 fl oz/¼ cup) lemon juice
1 pinch salt
1 pinch freshly ground black pepper
½ pinch cayenne pepper

Mix all of the ingredients together in a blender on minimum speed for 20 seconds.

SPICY MAYONNAISE

20 g (¾ oz) parmesan cheese
120 g (4¼ oz) Kewpie (Japanese) mayonnaise (Asian food stores)
30 g (1 oz) sriracha sauce
1 teaspoon lime juice
1 teaspoon sambal oelek (Asian food stores)

Finely grate the parmesan and mix vigorously with the rest of the ingredients.

SOY-MUSTARD SAUCE

50 g (1¾ oz) soy sauce
50 g (1¾ oz) mustard

Gradually whisk the soy sauce into the mustard.

SOY-GINGER SAUCE

470 ml (16½ fl oz) water
50 g (1¾ oz) fresh ginger
235 ml (8 fl oz) organic soy sauce

Bring the water to the boil with the ginger, peeled and sliced into rounds. Reduce the heat to a low simmer. Cover and cook for 20 minutes. Add the soy sauce and cook for another 5 minutes.

HONEY MUSTARD SAUCE

65 g (2¼ oz) mustard
100 g (3½ oz) honey
1 teaspoon thyme
30 g (1 oz) mustard seeds

Vigorously mix all the ingredients together. Place in the refrigerator.

LEMON CHILLI SAUCE

1 tablespoon freshly chopped ginger
2 tablespoons sriracha sauce (Asian food stores)
1 teaspoon salt
125 ml (4 fl oz/½ cup) lemon juice
125 ml (4 fl oz/½ cup) olive oil
1 teaspoon chives

Blend the sliced ginger, sriracha sauce and salt in a food processor, with enough lemon juice so they mix together. Pour in the olive oil, the rest of the lemon juice and the chives. Mix.

PONZU SAUCE

2 tablespoons soy sauce
1½ tablespoons dashi (home-made or from a cube, from Japanese food stores)
1 tablespoon lime juice
2 teaspoons rice vinegar
1 tablespoon mirin (Asian food stores)
1 tablespoon soft brown sugar

Mix together all of the ingredients and let it sit for at least 1 hour.

CHIPOTLE AIOLI

20 g (¾ oz) chipotle chillies in adobo sauce (in tins from specialty food stores)
1 garlic clove
40 g (1½ oz) tomato sauce (ketchup)
80 g (2¾ oz) mayonnaise

Mixed together the chopped chipotle chillies, the very finely chopped garlic, tomato sauce and mayonnaise until smooth.

TOMATO PIZZA SAUCE

500 g (1 lb 2 oz) whole peeled tomatoes (tinned)
½ onion
1 anchovy in oil (tinned)
2 tablespoons olive oil
1 tablespoon mixed dried herbs

Purée the tomatoes in a food processor, then bring to the boil with the chopped half onion and anchovy with a drizzle of olive oil. Reduce the heat to the lowest setting and cook for 1 hour, stirring regularly. Add the mixed herbs.

HARISSA

6 red capsicums (peppers)
480 ml (16½ fl oz) olive oil
2 tablespoons salt
3 tablespoons cumin seeds
1 tablespoon fennel seeds
1 tablespoon caraway seeds
1 tablespoon freshly ground black pepper
5 medium garlic cloves
2 tablespoons smoked paprika

Brush the capsicums with olive oil, sprinkle with 1 tablespoon salt, and cook in a 220°C (425°F) oven for 6 minutes. Place the whole spices on another baking tray and cook for another 6 minutes. Blend the cooled chopped roasted capsicums with the garlic in a food processor. Grind the toasted spices and add them to the capsicum purée with some paprika. Blend in a food processor until smooth. Add the remaining salt and the pepper and mix in slowly. Stir in the olive oil gradually until the colour lightens and the mixture is creamy.

HARISSA HOLLANDAISE

200 g (7 oz) butter
4 egg yolks
15 ml (½ fl oz) lemon juice
1 teaspoon mustard
1½ tablespoons harissa paste (tube)
1 pinch salt
1 pinch freshly ground black pepper

Melt the butter on a low heat, without stirring. Place the egg yolks in a saucepan. Place the saucepan on a very low heat (or over simmering water). Whisk the eggs for at least 5 minutes. The volume should at least double, without the eggs cooking, so no steam or smoke should appear. Incorporate the melted butter very gently, continuing to whisk. When the sauce has doubled in volume, add the lemon juice and mix it in. Add the mustard, harissa, salt and pepper, then mix.

VINAIGRETTE

2 tablespoons olive oil
1 tablespoon balsamic vinegar
1 teaspoon mustard
1 teaspoon honey
1 pinch salt
1 pinch freshly ground black pepper

Whisk the olive oil with the vinegar, add the mustard and mix, then add the honey and mix again. Season with salt and pepper.

LEMON VINAIGRETTE

125 ml (4 fl oz/½ cup) olive oil
60 ml (2 fl oz/¼ cup) wine vinegar
1 small bunch curly-leaf parsley
1 garlic clove
45 ml (1½ fl oz) lemon juice
30 g (1 oz) mustard
1 teaspoon oregano
½ teaspoon salt
½ teaspoon freshly ground black pepper

Emulsify the olive oil with the wine vinegar. Mix with the chopped parsley, crushed garlic and the rest of the ingredients, then transfer to a resealable container that can be used as a shaker. Shake vigorously before pouring over a salad.

CONDIMENTS
CONFIT GARLIC

Olive oil
24 garlic cloves

Pour enough olive oil into a saucepan to cover the peeled garlic cloves. Cook the cloves in the oil, kept at a bare simmer but under boiling point, for between 45 minutes and 1 hour. The cloves should be tender but not falling apart. Pour into a jar with a lid.

PICKLED GREEN CHILLIES

MAKES 1 JAR

1 garlic clove
400 ml (14 fl oz) white vinegar
200 g (7 oz) sugar
400 ml (14 fl oz) water
½ teaspoon salt
1 pinch cinnamon
1 pinch turmeric
3 bay leaves
200 g (7 oz) small green chillies

Crush the garlic and bring all the ingredients, except the chillies, to the boil in a saucepan on a medium heat. Add the chillies and cook, covered, on a low heat for 15 minutes. Pour into a glass jar. Cool at room temperature. It will be ready after 3 days and keeps for up to 1 week.

CUCUMBER & RADISH PICKLES

340 g (11¾ oz) cucumbers
200 g (7 oz) radishes
1 teaspoon salt
40 g (1½ oz) sugar
130 ml (4¼ fl oz) white vinegar
200 ml (7 fl oz) water

Slice the cucumbers and radishes into rounds, toss with the salt and let them drain for at least 1 hour, stirring after 30 minutes. Dissolve the sugar in the vinegar and water in a bowl. Put the drained vegetables into a jar, pour over the liquid and refrigerate for at least 24 hours.

PICKLED RED ONIONS

1 litre (35 fl oz/4 cups) red wine vinegar
3 garlic cloves
5 red onions

Pour the vinegar and garlic into a large saucepan on a medium heat, bring to the boil and cook for 5 minutes. Add the onions and bring back to the boil. Cook on a low heat, covered, for 10 minutes. Drain the onions, keeping the liquid. Place the onions in a bowl with the garlic, pour the liquid over and cool. Place in the refrigerator for at least 24 hours.

PICKLED CUCUMBERS

900 g (2 lb) small cucumbers
145 g (5 oz) kosher salt (American food stores)
480 ml (17 fl oz) white vinegar
480 ml (17 fl oz) cider vinegar
240 ml (8 fl oz) water
130 g (4½ oz) sugar
1 tablespoon cumin
1 tablespoon mustard seeds
1 teaspoon chilli powder

Slice the cucumbers into rounds. Combine all the other ingredients in a saucepan on a medium heat and bring to the boil. Continue stirring until the sugar has completely dissolved. Turn off the heat and allow to cool for 15 minutes. Pour the liquid over the cucumbers placed in a container or resealable jar. Let them stand for at least 4 hours and keep up to 2 days.

PICKLED WHITE ONIONS

70 ml (2¼ fl oz) white vinegar
70 ml (2¼ fl oz) water
160 g (5½ oz) onions
1 sprig thyme
1 pinch fennel seeds

Bring the vinegar, water, chopped onions, thyme and fennel seeds to the boil. Turn off the heat and allow to cool. Place the onions and liquid in a jar, consume within 2 days.

CORIANDER CHUTNEY

1 bunch coriander (cilantro)
1 handful cashews
1 small cube fresh ginger
1 red chilli
2 teaspoons salt
Juice of 1 lime

Blend all the ingredients together in a food processor.

ROASTED TOMATOES

5 tomatoes
2 tablespoons olive oil
2 garlic cloves
1 teaspoon oregano
½ teaspoon paprika
1 teaspoon thyme
2 bay leaves
1 tablespoon salt
¼ teaspoon freshly ground black pepper
½ teaspoon sugar

Preheat the oven to 160°C (315°F), then cut the tomatoes into quarters and remove the pulp and seeds and reserve. Pour over the olive oil and add the diced garlic and all the herbs, spices and sugar to the tomatoes. Make sure the tomatoes, skin and flesh, are well coated with the oil and seasonings. Transfer the tomatoes to a baking tray lined with baking paper. Pour over the reserved tomato pulp. Bake for about 45 minutes – stop cooking before the tomatoes start to collapse. When cool, transfer to a plastic container with a lid, and use within 3–4 days.

PEPPERCORN MIX

100 g (3½ oz/⅔ cup) black peppercorns
50 g (1¾ oz/⅓ cup) white peppercorns
25 g (1 oz) long pepper (gourmet delicatessens)
15 g (½ oz) pink peppercorns
10 g (¼ oz) sichuan peppercorns
Vegetable oil

Toast all of the peppercorns separately in a hot frying pan lightly brushed with vegetable oil for 2 minutes. Once they have cooled, mix them together and crush using a mortar and pestle.

SIDES
KALE SIDE

MAKES 1 SERVE

1 French shallot
1 garlic clove
2 tablespoons vegetable oil
135 g (4¾ oz) kale
500 ml (17 fl oz/2 cups) water
60 ml (2 fl oz/¼ cup) soy sauce
1 small piece fresh ginger
2 tablespoons sesame oil
1 handful pomegranate seeds

Sauté the finely chopped shallot and crushed garlic in the vegetable oil on a high heat for 3 minutes. Reduce the heat to medium, add the roughly chopped kale and cook for 3 minutes, stirring. Mix together the water, soy sauce, finely chopped ginger and sesame oil and pour into the frying pan. Cook for about 5 minutes, stirring, until the kale softens. Serve cold with the pomegranate seeds.

GUACAMOLE

4 avocados
1 lime
200 g (7 oz) tomatoes
40 g (1½ oz) onion
1 teaspoon cumin
1 teaspoon paprika
Tabasco sauce (or 1 green chilli)
½ bunch coriander (cilantro)
10 g (¼ oz) salt
½ teaspoon freshly ground black pepper
25 ml (¾ fl oz) olive oil

Mix together the mashed avocados, lime juice, diced tomatoes, chopped onion, cumin and paprika, 2–3 drops of Tabasco sauce (or the green chilli, seeded and very finely chopped) and the chopped coriander leaves. Season and pour in the olive oil.

REFRIED BEANS

450 g (1 lb) dried red kidney beans
2.8 litres (98 fl oz) water
2 teaspoons salt
1 bay leaf
2 onions
1 chicken stock cube
3 tablespoons lard or 30 ml (1 fl oz)
vegetable oil
3 garlic cloves
1 jalapeño

Soak the dried beans overnight in the water with the salt. The next day, rinse thoroughly to remove any small stones. Bring the water to the boil with the bay leaf, 1 chopped onion and the crumbled chicken stock cube. Reduce the heat and simmer very gently, covered, for about 2½ hours, or until the beans are tender and lose their skin. Remove the onion and bay leaf, drain the beans and keep the cooking liquid. Heat the lard on a high heat in a deep frying pan, add the crushed garlic, the other chopped onion and seeded and sliced jalapeño. Cook for about 3 minutes, stirring, until softened not browned. On a medium heat, add some of the cooked beans and 250 ml (9 fl oz/1 cup) of the cooking liquid. Mix together well. Mash the beans to the consistency of a dry purée. Cook for about 5 minutes longer. Repeat the process and season with salt and freshly ground black pepper.

RECIPES
CHILLI

50 ml (1½ fl oz) canola oil
900 g (2 lb) minced (ground) beef
180 g (6½ oz) onions
1 generous tablespoon finely
chopped garlic
3 tablespoons chilli powder
¾ teaspoon ground cumin
¼ teaspoon red chilli flakes
1 teaspoon oregano
120 g (4¼ oz) tomato paste
(concentrated purée)
2 beef stock cubes
550 g (1 lb 4 oz) drained red kidney
beans

Heat the canola oil on a medium heat in a large frying pan. Cook the minced beef, stirring, for 6 minutes, or until browned. Drain off the fat and transfer the cooked beef to a wide rondeau-style pan (a wide shallow saucepan). In the same frying pan you cooked the beef in, fry the diced onions and finely chopped garlic for 5 minutes. Take off the heat. Add the chilli powder, cumin, chilli flakes and oregano. Stir to mix through the garlic and onions well. Add the tomato paste. Return to the heat on a low temperature and stir for 5 minutes. Add 850 ml (29½ fl oz) beef stock, made up with the stock cubes, according to the instructions on the packet. Stir for another 2 minutes until well mixed. Transfer everything to the rondeau pan with the drained beef and season with salt and freshly ground black pepper. Bring everything to the boil on a medium heat. Reduce the heat to low, half-cover the pan and let it simmer for 1¼ hours. Add the drained beans, stir and cook for another 15 minutes.

TEMPURA PRAWNS
SERVES 1

40 g (1½ oz) plain (all-purpose) flour
40 g (1½ oz) cornflour (cornstarch)
1 egg yolk
½ teaspoon salt
½ teaspoon sugar
75 ml (2¼ fl oz) iced soda water (club
soda)
2 litres (70 fl oz/8 cups) peanut oil
200 g (7 oz) prawns (shrimp)

Mix together the flours, egg yolk, salt and sugar. Gradually mix in the iced soda water and stir vigorously. Heat the peanut oil in a deep-fryer or frying pan on a medium heat. Dip the prawns in the batter, then deep-fry each prawn for about 1½ minutes until golden brown. Drain each prawn on paper towel.

VINEGARED SUSHI RICE

6 sushi = 150 g (5½ oz); 1 maki = 25 g
(1 oz) rice ; 1 tango roll = between 4
and 6 maki
300 g (10½ oz) white rice
35 ml (1 fl oz) white rice vinegar
(Asian food stores)
1½ tablespoons sugar
1 pinch salt

Wash the rice three times in fresh water in a perforated pan. Let the rice rest for 40 minutes in cold water. Drain and let the rice dry for 10 minutes. Cook, covered, for 10 minutes on a high heat or until steam appears, then for 10 minutes on a low heat. In a small saucepan on a low heat, whisk together the vinegar, sugar and salt for 5 minutes, the sugar must be dissolved. Mix this liquid into the rice, stirring constantly, until the rice reaches room temperature.

FRIED EGGS

Heat some olive oil in a frying pan, add the egg white first, then the yolk when the white starts to simmer. Using a spatula, cover the yolk with the white, rotating the frying pan so that you make a ball. Place on paper towel.

POACHED EGGS

Place some plastic wrap in a small bowl and pour in a few drops of olive oil. Break the egg into the bowl and tie the plastic wrap into a knot on top to enclose the egg. Repeat the process for each egg to make four 'bulbs'. Fill a large saucepan two-thirds full with water and bring to the boil. Turn off the heat and wait for the bubbles to disappear. Place the four eggs in the water and let them cook for 3½ minutes. Remove the eggs from the water, then cut off the knot to remove the eggs without piercing them.

PIZZA DOUGH

MAKES 4 BASES

10 g (¼ oz) sugar
1 tablespoon treacle or molasses
450 ml (16 fl oz) water
10 g (¼ oz) fresh yeast (from bakery)
10 ml (¼ fl oz) olive oil
750 g (1 lb 10 oz) soft (T45) flour or plain (all-purpose) flour
15 g (½ oz) coarse salt

Dissolve the sugar and treacle in the water heated to 40°C (104°F), add the yeast and mix with your fingers. Pour 90 per cent of the oil into the water and mix for 1 minute. Add the flour and salt. Put the mixture into an electric standmixer and knead on low speed for about 3 minutes. Add the rest of the oil and knead on medium speed for 4 minutes. Divide the dough into four portions, knead and form into balls. Place each oiled ball in an oiled bowl, cover with plastic wrap and place in the refrigerator for 3 days. The dough is ready when you can see small dark fermentation bubbles.

CORNED BEEF

SERVES 2

1 kg (2 lb 4 oz) chuck or blade beef
THE BRINE
2 litres (70 fl oz/8 cups) water
2 teaspoons paprika
½ cinnamon stick
2 teaspoons freshly ground black pepper
2 teaspoons mustard seeds
2 teaspoons ground ginger
2 teaspoons chilli
4 teaspoons quatre-épices (French spice mix)
1 teaspoon dried thyme
3 garlic cloves, bruised
200 g (7 oz) coarse sea salt
100 g (3½ oz) soft brown sugar

Rinse and dry the beef. Make a few holes in the meat with a thin meat fork or large needle. For the brine: bring the water to the boil, add all of the brining ingredients and mix. Once the sugar and salt have dissolved, or after about 3 minutes, remove from the heat. Place the liquid in the refrigerator. Pour the cold liquid over the meat in a suitable deep, clear container or in a large zip-lock bag. The meat needs to be kept completely submerged for the whole time it is in the refrigerator. Use a small plate to keep the meat submerged if needed. Check the meat is still submerged every day. Leave in the refrigerator for between 10 days and 6 weeks.

DRINKS
HOME-MADE LEMONADE

MAKES 1 LITRE (35 FL OZ/4 CUPS)

3 tablespoons honey
750 ml (26 fl oz/3 cups) mineral water
250 ml (9 fl oz/1 cup) fresh lemon juice
2 or 3 sprigs mint

Bring the honey and 250 ml (9 fl oz/1 cup) of the water to the boil. Mix together and cool at room temperature, cover and place in the refrigerator. Mix the lemon juice (seeds removed but not the pulp) with the remaining water, then combine the two mixtures. Add some bruised mint leaves. Serve well chilled.

PACIFIC COAST HIGHWAY AND GETTY VILLA DR, MALIBU

ADDRESS BOOK

WEST LOS ANGELES

THE APPLE PAN
10801 W Pico Blvd, Los Angeles,
CA 90064, USA

SANTA MONICA

THAI DISHES
1910 Wilshire Blvd, Santa Monica,
CA 90403, USA

**SANTA MONICA SEAFOOD
MARKET & CAFÉ**
1000 Wilshire Blvd, Santa Monica,
CA 90401, USA

PINKBERRY
1456 3rd St, Promenade, Santa
Monica, CA 90401, USA

CORA'S COFFEE SHOPPE
1802 Ocean Ave, #B, Santa Monica,
CA 90401, USA

LA URBAN FITNESS
3015 Main St, Santa Monica,
CA 90405, USA

BRENTWOOD

A VOTRE SANTE
13016 San Vicente Blvd, Los
Angeles, CA 90049, USA

FARMSHOP
Brentwood Country Mart, 225 26th
St #25, Santa Monica, CA 90402,
USA

SAWTELLE

HARA SUSHI INC
12222 Wilshire Blvd #101,
Los Angeles, CA 90025, USA

DOWN TOWN LOS ANGELES

GRAND CENTRAL MARKET
317 S Broadway, Los Angeles,
CA 90013, USA

SPRINKLES CUPCAKES
735 S Figueroa St, Los Angeles,
CA 90017, USA

CALIFORNIA PIZZA KITCHEN
735 S Figueroa St #305, Los
Angeles, CA 90017, USA

IMPRESSO CAFE
1115 S Hope St, Los Angeles,
CA 90015, USA

**INTELLIGENTSIA COFFEE
COFFEEBAR**
3922 W Sunset Blvd, Los Angeles,
CA 90029, USA

CHINATOWN

PHILIPPE THE ORIGINAL
1001 N Alameda St, Los Angeles,
CA 90012, USA

UNIVERSITY PARK

JACKS N JOE
2498 S Figueroa St, Los Angeles,
CA 90007, USA

**LOS ANGELES TRADE-TECHNICAL
COLLEGE**
400 W Washington Blvd, Los
Angeles, CA 90015, USA

ART DISTRICT

ZINC CAFE & MARKET & BAR
580 Mateo St, Los Angeles,
CA 90013, USA

PIZZANISTA!
2019 E 7th St, Los Angeles,
CA 90021, USA

HERMOSA BEACH

PARADISE BOWLS
1246 Hermosa Ave, Hermosa
Beach, CA 90254, USA

ABIGAILE
1301 Manhattan Ave, Hermosa
Beach, CA 90254, USA

INGLEWOOD

PANN'S RESTAURANT
6710 La Tijera Blvd, Los Angeles,
CA 90045, USA

RANDY'S DONUTS
805 W Manchester Blvd,
Inglewood, CA 90301, USA

HUNTINGTON PARK

IN-N-OUT BURGER
6000 Pacific Blvd, Huntington
Park, CA 90255, USA

HOLLYWOOD

BEACHWOOD CAFE
2695 N Beachwood Dr, Los
Angeles, CA 90068, USA

**HOLLYWOOD FARMERS' MARKET
DTLA CHEESE / PRESS BROTHERS
JUICERY / EGGSLUT**
1600 Ivar Ave, Los Angeles, CA
90028, USA

THE OINKSTER HOLLYWOOD
776 Vine St, Los Angeles, CA
90038, USA

JOE'S PIZZA
6504 Hollywood Blvd, Los Angeles,
CA 90028, USA

BEVERLY

CANTER'S DELI
419 N Fairfax Ave, Los Angeles, CA 90036, USA

FREE RANGE
8400 Melrose Pl, West Hollywood, CA 90069, USA

JOAN'S ON THIRD
8350 W 3rd St, Los Angeles, CA 90048, USA

FAIRFAX

PINK'S HOT DOGS
709 N La Brea Ave, Los Angeles, CA 90039, USA

MELROSE TRADING POST
7850 Melrose Ave, Los Angeles, CA 90046, USA

STUDIO CITY

BARREL AND ASHES
11801 Ventura Blvd, Studio City, CA 91604, USA

BURBANK

CHILI JOHN'S
2018 W Burbank Blvd, Burbank, CA 91506, USA

LARRY'S CHILI DOG
3122 W Burbank Blvd, Burbank, CA 91505, USA

VENICE

KREATION KAFE & JUICERY
1202 Abbot Kinney Blvd, Venice, CA 90291, USA

KOMODO
235 Main St, Venice, CA 90291, USA

ABBOT'S PIZZA COMPANY
1407 Abbot Kinney Blvd, Venice, CA 90291, USA

GJELINA TAKE AWAY
1427 Abbot Kinney Blvd, Venice, CA 90291, USA

GJUSTA
320 Sunset Ave, Venice, CA 90291, USA

POKE-POKE
2011 Ocean Front Walk, Venice, CA 90291, USA

PLANT FOOD AND WINE
1009 Abbot Kinney Blvd, Venice, CA 90291, USA

1701 OCEAN FRONT WALK
1701 Ocean Front Walk, Venice, CA 90291, USA

MAR VISTA

MITSUWA MARKETPLACE SANTOUKA/SANUKI
3760 S Centinela Ave, Los Angeles, CA 90066, USA

VENTURA

THE FARMER AND THE COOK
339 W El Roblar Dr, Ojai, CA 93023, USA

MALIBU

NEPTUNE'S NET SEAFOOD RESTAURANT
42505 Pacific Coast Hwy, Malibu, CA 90265, USA

PACIFIC PALISADES

CAFFE' DELFINI
147 W Channel Rd, Santa Monica, CA 90402, USA

SILVER LAKE

NATUREWELL
3824 Sunset Blvd, Los Angeles, CA 90026, USA

TACOS DELTA
3806 Sunset Blvd, Los Angeles, CA 90026, USA

MORNINGS NIGHTS CAFE
1523 Griffith Park Blvd, Los Angeles, CA 90026, USA
NOW CLOSED

WESTLAKE

ORIGINAL TOMMY'S
2575 W Beverly Blvd, Los Angeles, CA 90057, USA

HIGHLAND PARK

KITCHEN MOUSE
5904 N Figueroa St, Los Angeles, CA 90042, USA

LOS FELIZ

ALCOVE CAFE & BAKERY
1929 Hillhurst Ave, Los Angeles, CA 90027, USA

INDEX

PICKLE (GHERKIN)
Salmon plate	186

PINEAPPLE
Kale jungle bowl	178
Spinach & pineapple juice	126
Vitality smoothie	56

PISTACHIO NUT KERNEL
Vegan lasagne	202

PIZZA
BBQ chicken pizza	132
Guanciale pizza	182
Kale pizza	34
Mac & cheese pizza	84
Pizza dough	262
Salad pizza	168
Thai chicken pizza	52

PLANT MILK
Multigrain porridge	190

PLANT PROTEIN POWDER
Muscle Beach Venice smoothie	18

POLENTA (CORNMEAL)
Hoecake	154

POMEGRANATE
Frozen yoghurt	20

PORCHETTA
Porchetta sandwich	180

PORK
Pork ramen	208
Tacos al pastor	234

POTATO
Chicken wings hash brown	100
Eggs Benedict	103
Guacamole & cheddar fries hot dog	146
Mulligatawny soup	212

PRAWN (SHRIMP)
Cioppino (fish and seafood stew)	22
Corona maki roll	42
Prawn pad thai	30
Prawn tacos	170
Tango maki roll	40
Tempura prawns	261

PROVOLONE CHEESE
Egg-kale open sandwich	184

QUINOA
Fez bowl	120
Multigrain porridge	190

RADISH
Avocado & radish toast	80
Banh-mi chicken taco	172
Cucumber & radish pickles	259

RAPINI (BROCCOLI RABE)
Porchetta sandwich	180

RASPBERRY
Muscle Beach Venice smoothie	18

RED KIDNEY BEANS
Chilaquiles	236
Chilli spaghetti bowl	156
Huevos rancheros	250
Refried beans	261

RED WINE
Sangria	220

RICE
Chicken breakfast burrito	14
Chilaquiles	236
Corona maki roll	42
Gomasio brown rice cakes	248
Mulligatawny soup	212
Mushroom bowl	194

RICE (continued)
Sophia bowl	116
Tacos al pastor	234
Tango maki roll	40
Vinegared sushi rice	262
Veggie burger & kale side	122
Veggie garden wrap	32

RICE PAPER
Corona maki roll	42

RICOTTA CHEESE
Avocado-pesto-ricotta toast	62
Avocado toast	54
Mac & cheese pizza	84

ROLLED (PORRIDGE) OATS
Granola	196
Multigrain porridge	190
Parfait	246
Porridge	114

SAGE
Fried chicken sandwich	98

SAKE
Sake bomb	44

SAUERKRAUT
Corned beef Reuben sandwich	136

SESAME SEED
Corona maki roll	42
Gomasio brown rice cakes	248
Granola	196
Parfait	246

SMOKED SALMON
Salmon open sandwich	184
Salmon plate	186

SOY SAUCE
Ponzu sauce	258
Soy-ginger sauce	258
Soy-mustard sauce	258

SPAGHETTI
Chilli spaghetti bowl	156

SPINACH (ENGLISH)
Eggs Benedict	103
Kale jungle bowl	178
Spinach & pineapple juice	126
Vegan lasagne	202
Veggie garden wrap	32
Vitality smoothie	56

SPRING ONION (SCALLION)
Beef udon	209
Pork ramen	208
Prawn pad thai	30
Thai chicken pizza	52

SRIRACHA
Lemon chilli sauce	258
Spicy mayonnaise	258

STRAWBERRY
Acai breakfast bowl	90
Fried chicken sandwich & spicy strawberry jam	138
Frozen yoghurt	20
Granola breakfast bowl	230
Strawberry lemonade	150
Strawberry smoothie	88

SUNFLOWER SEED
Granola	196
Parfait	246

SWEET POTATO
Mulligatawny soup	212

SWORDFISH
Swordfish sliders	26

TABASCO SAUCE
Buffalo sauce	257

TAHINI
Tahini sauce	258

TOFU
Sophia bowl	116

TOMATO
Avocado cheeseburger	160
BBQ chicken pizza	132
Chicken breakfast burrito	14
Chilaquiles	236
Chilli cheeseburger	240
Cioppino (fish and seafood stew)	22
Double cheeseburger	108
Egg-kale open sandwich	184
Eggs Benedict	103
Grilled cheese with tomato	144
Guacamole	260
Guanciale pizza	182
Huevos rancheros	250
Mushroom bowl	194
Prawn tacos	170
Roasted tomatoes	260
Salad pizza	168
Swordfish sliders	26
Tomato pizza sauce	258
Vegan lasagne	202
Veggie burger & kale side	122
Veggie garden wrap	32
Zucchini spaghetti bolognese	222

TOMATO SAUCE (KETCHUP)
Barbecue sauce	257
Chipotle aioli	258
Russian sauce	257
Smoky tomato sauce	258
Spreading sauce	257

TORTILLA
Banh-mi chicken taco	172
Chicken breakfast burrito	14
Chicken-cheese pitta	126
Chilaquiles	236
Huevos rancheros	250
Kimchi nachos	174
Prawn tacos	170
Tacos al pastor	234
Veggie garden wrap	32

TRUFFLE CHEESE
Asparagus & mushroom focaccia	188

TUNA
Hawaiian tuna poke	200

VANILLA (EXTRACT AND BEAN)
Banana cream pie	70
French toast	102
Multigrain porridge	190
Parfait	246
Porridge	114
Vanilla cupcakes	50

VANILLA ICE CREAM
Hot fudge sundae	152

VEAL
Zucchini spaghetti bolognese	222

WAKAME
Beef udon	209

WALNUTS
Avocado-pesto-ricotta toast	62
Kale side	122
Porridge	114

WHITE FISH
Cioppino (fish and seafood stew)	22

ZUCCHINI (COURGETTE)
Vegan lasagne	202
Veggie garden wrap	32
Zucchini spaghetti bolognese	222

RECIPE INDEX

ROADWAY INN. VINE ST

GREETINGS FROM LOS ANGELES

Adèle, I see you in every photo I take. Thank you for all those little things you did for me. Adrian, thank you for taking over the reins and letting me live this adventure. You are always correct. Julie, without you, this project would never have seen the light. During all those hours of work, you always stayed motivated, funny and inspired. Fahd, for your proofreading and motivation. Your confidence in me gave me strength. Claudio and Mooms, for always being ready to listen. Jean-Michel, you have always shown me the path to find mine, and you are always there for me. Thank you for your numerous re-readings and your beautiful way with words. GeeGee, you gave me so much inspiration in photography. Your gift, last year, touched me a great deal. Thank you for always being there for me. Maria, you are such a beautiful model of courage. As soon as things go wrong, I remember it. Chrystou, you are always there to listen. Clarisse, I admire your courage and your listening, you are extraordinary. Albane, I hope you like this book, I would love to go there with you. Rose, you are an angel, thank you for your good advice. I hope you will soon discover the City of Angels. Gonze, that Texas was unforgettable. Thank you for your good advice, you always take care of me. Val, thank you for supporting, advising, helping and motivating me through this whole adventure and in fact since forever. Palominos, thank you for your eye on the photos. Lisa, when you aren't preventing me from doing something stupid, you are giving me good ideas. Arturo, I can't wait for you to share with me a little of everything you know about silver chloride and for us to spend some time together. You are my source of inspiration on a daily basis. Janine, thank you for always listening and always finding the right word.

Norbert, for always being flexible and for your talent. Limon, for having eaten so many of our test donuts. Deborah, you found me the impossible to find. Anna, for your pseudo smoothie tests and inspiration. Élodie, Alexandra, Anna, Didier and Axelle, every day, I wonder if I will wake up and find it's all a dream. Thank you for being there. Michel, thank you for always being there for me and having introduced me to Adrian. You are a model of courage. Jeannine, thank you for your support and the calm you inspire in me. Pierre-Édouard, sorry once again for that stupid oversight. I still feel angry with myself about it. Rémy, for your expertise in focaccia and for always being there for us. Sorry Pieter for my silence. I have missed you. Sorry about that Simon, can't wait to go climbing again! Without you Yves-Marie, this book would never have seen the light. Sorry, Antoine and Labuche, I can't wait to get back to our little routines. Sorry, Ombeline, for my absence, I missed you a lot. Cécile, for all the time you spent re-reading and correcting me, always with the same good humour. Cécile for your time, your list, and for sharing your Los Angeles with me. And for introducing me to Moni and Samanta. Samanta and Moni, thank you for your time and your list! Chad, I'm sorry I missed your birthday. Julien, you are a real source of inspiration in everything you do: long live Phamilyfirst! Jackie and Nathalie, thanks for caring since day 1. You're always around, I love you guys. Aymeric, for your friendship, your list, your advice and the good times we had in Los Angeles. Colin, those who love us, never really leave us. La Chantre, thank you for your advice, I always listened to you. TLF, happy birthday again I love you, best man I know. Étienne, Olive, Biloute, you are role models, I hope you like this book. Maya, Charlotte, Caro, they are lucky. Arthur, for your list and the good moments. Jerry, without whom Blend would never have seen the light, nor this book. Thank you, you are a daily inspiration. Laurence and Olivier, I missed you. Maria, for your encouragement, your good humour and for having made Jerry even more awesome. Rita, without whom this book would never have seen the light. Emmanuel at Marabout for your good plans and these wonderful journeys. Élisabeth, at Marabout, you saved my behind and always listened. Pauline, at Marabout, aka Wonder Woman. You helped me through each step with always the right word. And you were always there. Rose-Marie, at Marabout, for your open-mindedness and this good idea. Pascale, at Marabout, you support me every time I walk into your office. Nicolas, for your sharp eye and your help in sorting the photos. Laure, for your help and your jokes. Laure, for your advice and formidable eye. Philippe, for your inspiration and friendship. Aurore, Jeanne and Laurianne at Minsk Studio, for your support and beautiful work. Yan

and his mother, for your precious help reinterpreting that 100% L.A. dish, being alcohol-free and decaf. Nicks Pizza, 24 Rue du Faubourg Montmartre, Paris, and Nicholas, for your time, your help for the pizza dough and your trust. You make the best pizzas! Noglu Paris, for your help and hospitality. Indra alias Francis, for your readthroughs. Guillaume, thank you for your friendship and relaxing effect. Your advice is precious. Sarah, Brian and Jeff at Farmshop. Joan, Susie, Carol and Todd, at Joan's on Third. Alice Waters, for having sown the seeds and written the first lines of the California cuisine we benefit from today. Henry, at Thai Dishes. Michelle, at The Oinkster. John, at Zinc Cafe, for your hospitality, your time and precious advice. Sheela, Erika, Maggie and Thomas, at Komodo. Doc Guthrie at the Los Angeles Trade Technical College and all your team, including Roxanne. Your talented and welcoming students. Margaret, Arleene and Gene, from the Neptune's Net. Bashar, at À Votre Santé. Kristen, Natalie and Mollie, at Kreation Organic. Kenny, Michael and Matt at Barrel & Ashes. Michael, Dave and your friend at The Stronghold LA. Andy, at GM Leather for your custom pieces and the gifts. Stew and Kevin, from the Burgerlords. Jonathan Gold, for what you have done for Los Angeles. Patrick, at Pann's. Mike, Jason & Shayyan, Poke-Poke customers. Beth and your beautiful bike, in Venice. Vianney and your team at Jacks N Joe. Patti, from the Beachwood Cafe, for your generosity, your time and all those little stories about Hollywood. Derrick, at the Santa Monica Liquor Store. Erika, at Kitchen Mouse. Darren, his manager Ann, Gabriel and Ethan, at the Paradise Bowl. Thank you for your time Darren, I have rarely eaten so well as at your place. Anna, for letting me take a photo of her legs. Mariah, Christina, Steve and Levy, at the Melrose Trading Post. Johnny and his dog in a sidecar, at Brentwood Market. Aaron and Juliana, at the Golden Mean, for introducing me to MACA. Shelley, Alex, Christiane, Greg and Travis, at Gjusta and GTA. You are extraterrestrial beings. Be careful on the road, Greg! Alec, Debbie and Anthony, from Chili John's. Mara, at Caffe Luxxe. Brecia, at Grand Central Market. Turtle, Steven and Danny, at the Belvedere Skatepark. Candice and Kecho, surfers at Venice Beach. Stef, Alex, Gmuminski, Ryan and Bill, skateboarders at Venice Beach. Richard at Little Dom's. Karen and Nadja, for your introduction at Plant Food and Wine. And your friends, Juliana and Lily. Leigh at Plant Food and Wine. Steven, Olivia, Nicole, Johnny, Jaime and Hola, at The Farmer and the Cook. Anthony and Gilberto, at Cora's Coffee Shoppe. Juliette, from the Mart Barber Shop. Celia and Samir, from the Country Mart & Shoe Repair. Tony, Monica and Paco, at Naturewell. The Gonzalez family at Tacos Delta for your kindness and talent. Hardeep, from the Berlin Currywurst. Jeff and Ethan at Eggslut. To Whitney and Muriel, who were patient with me at Grand Central Market. Alex, from Caffe' Delfini, for taking care of me. And his partner, Gianpetro. Stefani at Santa Monica Seafood for your hospitality and the photos you secretly took of me! Yukarie and Matsuhisa Nobuyuki, at Nobu. Thom and Alex at Iron & Resin. Brian and Alison, for welcoming me into your home. Vera and Marilu, at Pink's. El Rey brother JD from El Rey's Garage, for that unforgettable moment. Dom, from D.C. Custom Designs, for the address of the swap meet at Veteran's Stadium. John and Veronica, at Larry's Chili Dog. Anthony at One Life Natural Food. David and Thomas, at Abigaile. Sean, at Alcove Cafe and Bakery. Vaughn, for all the time you spent looking for vintage postcards at Melrose Trading Post. The teams at The ICON LA laboratory for saving part of my film exposed to daylight. Scott, Max and all the cooks at Hara Sushi for sharing some of your secrets with me. Molly, at Mendocino Farm. Whole Foods. The Coffee Bean & Tea Leaf on Wilshire Blvd and 9th, in Santa Monica, where I made decisions that made me happy. Grant, at Cars with Class. Andrew and Mike, from the Santa Monica Farmers' Market. Kacey, Alex and Paolo, at Tanner Goods. Peter, the taxi driver photographer. Jordan, aka idratherbeshooting, a photographer I met at the Hollywood Farmers' Market. Juliann, at Mornings Nights. Sal and Guilver, from the LA Urban Fitness Center. Hector, who I met in Gjusta. Matthew Kinney. Google Maps and Google Earth, which allowed me to find so many destinations. And to find some again. To Dupon Images laboratory for the care you take developing my films. Sandrine especially for your welcome each time I come back from my travels. Jean-Marc, Dominique, Hervé and Laurent, at the Leica Store Beaumarchais. Panajou Bordeaux, for your efficiency.

Published in 2017 by Murdoch Books, an imprint of Allen & Unwin.
First published by Hachette Livre (Marabout) in 2016.

Murdoch Books Australia
83 Alexander Street
Crows Nest NSW 2065
Phone: +61 (0) 2 8425 0100
Fax: +61 (0) 2 9906 2218
murdochbooks.com.au
info@murdochbooks.com.au

Murdoch Books UK
Ormond House
26–27 Boswell Street
London WC1N 3JZ
Phone: +44 (0) 20 8785 5995
murdochbooks.co.uk
info@murdochbooks.co.uk

For Corporate Orders & Custom Publishing, contact our Business Development Team at salesenquiries@murdochbooks.com.au.

Publisher: Corinne Roberts
Layout: Minsk Studio Julie Dubos and Fahd El Jaoudi assisted by Aurore Guyet
Production: Lou Playfair

© Hachette Livre (Marabout) 2016

The moral rights of the author have been asserted.

A cataloguing-in-publication entry is available from the catalogue of the National Library of Australia at nla.gov.au.

ISBN 978 1 76052 272 8 Australia
ISBN 978 1 76052 774 7 UK

A catalogue record for this book is available from the British Library.

Printed by C & C Offset Printing Co. Ltd., China

TECHNICAL NOTE:
All of the photos were taken with analog Leica M series cameras with 24, 35, 50 and 90 mm lenses and the invaluable assistance of the 307 Billingham bag. The films used are Fujichrome VELVIA 50 / PROVIA 100F / PORTRA 160 & 400. The film was carefully developed by Dupon Images (74 Rue Joseph-de-Maistre, 75018 Paris) & The ICON LA.

N. SANTA MONICA BLVD & N. BEVERLY DRIVE